CW01198201

QE2 DIVA

Mary Mastony

MINERVA PRESS
LONDON
MONTREUX LOS ANGELES SYDNEY

QE2 DIVA
Copyright © Mary Mastony 1997

All Rights Reserved

No part of this book may be reproduced in any form,
by photocopying or by any electronic or mechanical means,
including information storage or retrieval systems,
without permission in writing from both the copyright owner
and the publisher of this book.

ISBN 1 86106 554 X

First Published 1997 by
MINERVA PRESS
195 Knightsbridge
London SW7 1RE

Printed in Great Britain
Antony Rowe Ltd, Chippenham, Wiltshire

QE2 DIVA

Dedication

To my loving parents, Frank and Julia
and
my very special brother, Michael

Special Tributes

CAPTAINS

Captain Arnott
  Captain Portet
    Captain Bennell
      Captain and Mrs Woodall
        Captain and Mrs Burton-Hall

MEDICAL OFFICERS

Doctor Roberts   Doctor Eardley

CRUISE PERSONNEL

Peter Longley   Elaine Mackay
Lindsay Frost   Maureen Ryan

MASTERS OF CEREMONIES

Paul Hopley   Colin Parker   Richard Parker
David Price   Jim Bowen   Andrew Graham

PIANO ACCOMPANISTS

Colin Brown   Ashley Stanton   Madeline Maxwell
Francis Heilbut   David Moore   Keith Ansell   Naki Ataman

OPERA TEACHERS

Inge Biosevas   Dr Jacklyn Schneider   Dr Valerie Goodall

ENTERTAINERS

Debbie and Steve McCormick   Christine and Mark Joyce

TRAVEL AGENTS

Doreen White   Lillian Musmanno   Dorothy Reminick

PASSENGERS

Mr and Mrs Jefford and Sarah Carol Walker Diana Gibson
Mr and Mrs Doreen Allen   Linda Hunt Lady Ann D'Winstanly
James and Margaret Craig

FAMILY

Michael and Doris Mastony   Julia and Edward Lynch
Tara Lynch   Frank and Helen Mastony   Sal McNamara
Pat and Florrie Griffin and Elenora and Peter

FRIEND

Lawrence Pergola Jr

COMPUTER TECHNICIAN

Friend and Spiritual Support
Elaine Martinelli

Contents

One	Traveling Solo: Paris, Orient Express, London 1985	11
	La Vie en Rose by Louiguy	
Two	Iberian Cruise 1986	25
	Nel Cor Pui Non Mi Sento Arietta by Paisiello	
Three	Lisbon, Gibraltar, Pria da Rocha 1987	43
	O Mio Babbino Caro by Puccini	
Four	Norwegian Fjord Cruise 1988	58
	Quando Me'n Vo Soletta by Puccini	
Five	Scandinavian Cruise 1989	75
	Caro Nome by Verdi	
Six	Cunard Line's 150th Anniversary 1990 The Royal Review and visit on board by Her Majesty Queen Elizabeth 2	92
	Il Bacio by L Arditi	
Seven	Tours of London and Paris 1991	113
	O Mio Babbino Caro, Caro Nome	
Eight	Caribbean Cruise 1992	129
	Un Bel Di Vedremo by Verdi London 1992	
Nine	World Cruise, Last Segment 1993	146
	Si Mi Chiamino Mimi by Puccini	

Ten	Norway and North Cape 1993	164
	Caro Nome, Un Bel Di, Si Mi Chiamino Mimi	
Eleven	Caribbean 1994	178
	O Mio Babbino Caro, Caro Nome	
Twelve	Scotland Tall Ships and North Cape and Fjords 1995	193
	O Mio Babbino Caro, Caro Nome, Un Bel Di	

STANDING OVATION

Chapter One
Traveling Solo: Paris, Orient Express, London 1985

Hello *QE2* travelers and friends. Let us enjoy together some favorite moments aboard the world's most wonderful ocean liner. We are the passengers who like to consider the super liner our second home. I have been traveling on board every summer for the last ten years. Ten summers of great memories. Each of those years I returned and composed albums of items and pictures of the trip. That is what this book is all about. Enjoy and recall!

The quote of my life, from my brother Michael: "When are you going to unravel all that yarn you wrap around yourself?" He was referring to my piano playing, singing and getting involved in new projects in which I become intensely interested. Now I am about to embark on the uncharted sea of writing this *QE2* saga. BON VOYAGE!

*

It was the spring of 1985 when the idea of traveling became foremost in my mind. I was just about to complete a course in French. My professor, a native of France, made the course so interesting that I knew I wanted to go to Paris to prove I could actually use the language I had studied. I had been to Paris with my family, but now I was going to attempt it alone. Believe me, the thought of it was too exciting to comprehend.

The premises of the travel agency that I consulted were on the route that led to where I had been taking the French classes.

The travel agent listened as I mapped out my proposed itinerary. It was quite complicated. I did not want to fly. I had flown before with my family, but for this trip I wanted to sail. Sail, that is, with the destination of Paris in mind. Also, at some point I wanted to travel on the Orient Express. Could she set up a schedule for this kind of trip? It was a fun challenge. She drew up a schedule that would take me on the ship *Queen Elizabeth II*. I was not familiar with this ship, but I was ready to find out about it. What I found out looked good to me. I had traveled with my parents on ocean liners, so I was familiar with ocean travel. This, however, would be different because I would be alone. I was depending on my travel agent to make the right plans. She did that and very well. Since she was from London, she knew the best hotels for me.

She scheduled to have me leave New York and arrive in Southampton. Then I would go by bus to Portsmouth where, at eleven o'clock at night, I would take a boat to Le Havre. On the boat I would have a cabin since it was an overnight trip. Then, when I arrived in Le Havre, I would take a train to Paris. Phew! Already it seemed unbelievable. In Paris, I would stay at the Regina hotel for three days and then travel by way of the Orient Express to London. There I would have three days to tour around London. Then, I would get aboard the *Queen Elizabeth II* and return to the United States. Could I do this? Alone?

My greatest fear, besides being on such a grand ship alone, was the fact that I would be out at eleven o'clock at night on the pier in Le Havre, France. Was it safe?

I began preparing for the voyage. One thing I was sure of was that I would take only one bag. That bag would be of a soft material in order to be as light and comfortable as possible. The trip would take a least sixteen days. I would need to be very careful to remember all the essentials for that period of time. I would wear a softly tailored suit. I had a soft light lavender shoulder bag with matching belt. I had my soft navy blue travel bag, I had my ticket, my passport and a smile to cover my feeling of anxiety.

My point of departure was my brother's home. Yes, I needed all the confidence I could get. His wife gave me support by saying that Regis Philbin, a TV host, would be on the very same ship. He was a very popular talk show host on American television. To say the least, it would be nice to see him in person. Well, I had been given an incentive!

The limousine arrived to take me to the pier in New York. We said our goodbyes. I was on my way! In my bag I had pictures of my mother and father. I had my passport ready. I had my camera. I knew that I would be taking pictures of all the wonderful sights I would see on such a trip.

I arrived at the pier where the *QE2* was berthed. The great ship looked fabulous. I was Alice in Wonderland. Three officers were in the waiting area. They smiled and I asked if I could have a picture. They were happy to oblige. As I continued forward, I had to have my picture taken in front of a Cunard sign indicating what was needed to get on board. I had my passport. I had my ticket, so, on I went. Four string instrumentalists serenaded the new passengers. I was delighted! Music has always been my greatest interest in life. How wonderful to hear it as I, albeit with apprehension, approached this great ship.

On board! What an exciting feeling! At the entrance to the Midships Lobby you are greeted by a host and hostess. Then you are given directions to your cabin. My cabin was on level four. I found my room without any trouble. It was a cozy room with a porthole. I had carried my travel bag on board so that I would not need to wait and endure more anxieties. Quickly, I reached into my bag and put my mother and father's picture on the dresser. I also put up the bon voyage cards that I had received before I left. Then I went on deck to watch as we departed. I looked wistfully at the receding skyline and wondered if I would ever see it again! I had made a call to my brother and his wife to let them know that I had arrived at the pier. Now, on deck, I was on my own!

In one of the main rooms a line was forming. What was going on? I learned that you had to get in line to find out where you would be having your meals. I got in line. I was assigned table 587 in the Tables of the World restaurant. Since, by this time, I was getting hungry, I chose the earliest serving. We were then allowed to enter and have a lunch. Not all of the passengers at my table had arrived but I was ready! My table was great! It overlooked the ocean. I was the only one there at that sitting. However, my waiter was so nice, I didn't feel lonesome. Already I had a waiter take a picture. This was an event, was it not? I was thrilled with everything and we hadn't sailed far. Off to a good start!

It was time to explore this beautiful ship. I knew exactly what I was looking for. Prior to taking this trip, I had read in the newspaper that there were eight grand pianos on board. All eight of the pianos were tuned when the ship arrived in New York. Very interesting! Well, I set out to find the pianos and generally look over this great ship. I play the piano and had recently taken part in some recitals. So now I busied myself by going about the ship looking for the grand pianos. I found one white one in the Midships Lobby. Actually I had spied it as I came aboard! I found one near the Midships Bar, next to the giant puzzle that is kept for puzzle aficionados. I found one in the Grand Lounge. This is the large entertainment room that has a modest stage for performers. It also had a spiral staircase that travelers will need to remember because it is no longer there as I write. I found one in the Lido. This was a beautiful domed room with swimming pool, palm trees, a bar, and tables in cozy little corners. One corner had neon lights behind it representing New York's skyline. The other cozy corner – there were two – had neon lights on the wall behind it representative of London. I liked these two places. Also there was a dance floor, which I found out later had twinkle lights showing through. To continue my search for pianos, I found one in a beautiful room called the Queen's Room. There was one also in the Yacht Club. There was a grand piano on stage in the theater on this huge ocean liner, I felt lucky to have found five on my preliminary survey of my new surroundings in which I would be spending five glorious days. The other three pianos I did locate later. However, five grand pianos seemed adequate to me.

Dinner time! This was the time to remove my traveling suit and get into something appropriate for my first dinner at sea. My small blue travel bag was unpacked. I had some choice. It was remarkable how much I had in that bag. By the way, on subsequent trips, I was never again to be so limited in what I packed. This time I selected a simple cotton dress. It looked like the right dress to be worn with a pair of blue, backless high heels. It was so exciting. Tonight my table companions would show up. Also, a daily schedule had been placed on my dresser. There was going to be a glittering show in the Grand Lounge. My fear was gradually subsiding. The sea was calm. I would take a glance out at it through the porthole. All was serene. All was well!

The first evening at sea went well. I did not keep a diary. However, from my album I find that I had two nice ladies at my table. There was room for more. That evening there was a show scheduled. Dancers danced in beautiful sequined gowns. It was splendid to look at. All had gone well with my first day at sea.

The first night in my cabin was an event. I had brought a two-piece nightgown set. It was new. Happily exhausted, I slipped into it. Would you believe it, this was so momentous that I had to take a picture? I didn't know exactly how to take a time shot on my camera. However, I quickly learned. The outcome was a happy "me" in a *QE2* cabin. I'm sure I slept like a charm.

Day two: I had slept well. My usual awakening time is six o'clock. This morning I was awakened by the sound of the daily program being slipped under my door. Wonderful! What would be on the agenda for the day? Regis Philbin was going to be interviewed by the ship's directress. That would be interesting. Perhaps I could get his autograph. Later he would address the passengers in the theater. It all came to pass. I was not only able to get an autograph, but I was able to talk to him and get a picture of us together. How proud I would be to show that picture to my sister-in-law!

That same evening I met some girls who were attending a girls' college. It was in New York close to Columbia University where I received my Masters Degree in Psychology. We laughed and had fun. They said that they didn't like their assigned table and asked if they could come to my table. They received permission. Now there would be five at table 587.

The next day a cocktail party was held in the Queen's Room. It was a time for passenger glitter. I didn't have glitter but I did have a pretty silk dress which was appropriate. It was a lovely party. We were introduced to the Captain, Robert

Arnott, and all of his officers. I began to feel I was part of a family.

The next day I met the social directress, Elaine Mackay. We had a lot in common since she had also been a school teacher. She invited me and another passenger for a cool drink. We had cokes! She knew how apprehensive I was about sailing. She very nicely calmed my fears, I will always remember her kindness. It is always a pleasure to see her on board whenever I sail. Thank you, Elaine.

I went to see the shopping area. There were some fabulous stores. I was fascinated by the beautiful formal gowns. I didn't have one in my bag, but I sure thought it would be nice to have one. There was a beautiful black gown that I liked. What a surprise! The sales lady said that I could take it to my room to try on. Lovely. I went to my room with it, I tried it on. It fit beautifully. Sooooooooo... I took a picture of myself in it. Dreamer that I am. No, I didn't buy the gown. It was too expensive!

The time actually came to re-pack my small bag. I had made some fine friends and enjoyed myself immensely. More was yet to come, because I would be making a return trip in about seven days. It was time to disembark. This would be, shall we say, exciting, for lack of a better word. I went to the travel bureau on the ship and they gave me some instructions about getting to France. Regis Philbin and his wife were also there inquiring about a flight to Paris. I was told that I would be taking a bus to Portsmouth. I would stop on the way there to have lunch. All of this was courtesy of the Cunard Line. I was strong. I could do this. After all, I would be seeing Paris!

At the pier in Southampton, I looked for the line that was captioned FERRY PASSENGERS. There I would give my ticket to get the bus to Portsmouth. There were not many of us there. However, the lady who took my ticket said that she would be accompanying us to Portsmouth. How wonderful! I would not be alone!

We boarded a bus and I found that I was seated next to the ticket lady. Wonderful! The others aboard were athletic-looking men. The ticket lady and I talked as we were being driven. Surprise of surprises, her name was Elizabeth Taylor. Not the Elizabeth Taylor of film fame, but interesting, to say the least, and a name that I would remember. As a matter of interest, something I could not know at the time, I was to see her again and again every year that I landed in Southampton. That is each of the ten years that I returned to England on my summer vacations. I would always be surprised to see her and greet her!

On the way to Le Havre, the Cunard bus stopped at the Albany hotel for our lunch break. This was courtesy of the Cunard Line. I thank them. At the table, I sat between two of those athletic men. They turned out to be motorcyclists who were going to do some cross country motorcycle riding through France. I was impressed. They gave me a straw cowboy sun hat they had bought, as they left. Merci beaucoup!

Elizabeth stayed with me all the way to Portsmouth. I found out that she was from the town of Lymington, England. I had been there with my brother and his family when we had flown over to tour England. I had liked the town very much. That time we stayed overnight in the Stanwell House hotel. On subsequent trips I had the opportunity to revisit the city. Elizabeth Taylor stayed with me until the ferry arrived and I embarked. Surely I never thought I would see her again. Thank you very, very much Elizabeth!

On the ferry, I had been booked in to a single cabin. I did not need to spend the night on deck, which some apparently had to do. The short trip was uneventful. It was at the moment of stepping on to French soil that I really felt alone. However, I ran for the train that was near the disembarking pier. I noticed the motorcyclists not far behind. The trip was also uneventful. However, I heard there had been a train wreck at one of the crossings that we were approaching. The law of averages consoled me. It couldn't happen again!

I arrived at the Paris train station. Here, I was to use my limited French. I called out, "Taxi, s'il vous plait!" Oh, I would have to tell Madame Christian, my French teacher, about that bit of outstanding linguistic ability. She would be so proud of me! The taxi took me to the Regina hotel in the heart of Paris.

The Regina hotel was a lovely quiet hotel. My travel agent had picked out exactly the kind of hotel that I would like. It was very expensive. However, I had wanted something safe and near the center of Paris. It was all of that. The lobby was a wine-red plush-carpeted room. I was delighted to see a grand piano in the corner of the main room. I would get to play the piano I was sure. I was taken to my room on the second floor. The bellboy opened the window of the room and to my delight I could see the Eiffel Tower. Splendid!

Now what to do? Well, very conveniently placed next door to me was a city tour office. Upon my arrival, it was still early morning, I decided to have lunch at the hotel and then inquire about a tour. Great! There was a city tour. I could see all of this famous city and take some good pictures. This I did. We were taken through Notre Dame cathedral and given a ride and historical summary of the city. Then we returned to the place where we had started, which was close to my hotel.

It had been a wonderful afternoon. I even found a letter from my friend Larry, who knew that I would be at that hotel at that time. It was reassuring. I ended the afternoon with an early dinner. Then, back to the tour office next door. It was, oh, so convenient! I selected the Moulin Rouge show to be my evening's entertainment. The price for one was ninety-eight American dollars. I was not afraid because I would be escorted by others and I would be returned directly to my hotel. Was it naughty? I would find out.

The Moulin Rouge or Red Mill as we Americans would call it, was approached by bus. I could see the neon lights in red in the shape of a windmill. This was it! The famous Moulin Rouge! Inside it was a very Parisian-looking theater, as you might well have imagined. There were red carpets, dim lights, and French-sounding music.

I was anxious for the show to begin. It did and it was entertaining. The show girls wore a covering of beige net that had a special effect. However, the music, the dancing, the feather costumes, the occasional comic acts, made it an evening of fine entertainment. During the intermission we were served various types of cheese.

After the show was over we were taken to a restaurant and served onion soup. It was about two o'clock in the morning when we were returned to our hotels. All was fine. However, it was at that time that I had my one and only, moment of real fear. When I got off the bus to enter my hotel, I found that the door was locked. I knocked at the window. There was no answer. Furthermore, there was a curtain over the window and I could not be seen! What to do? I happened to see another door. I would try that one. Well, thank goodness, it was opened by the doorman. I was safe!

When I got into my room that night I called my brother and his wife who were vacationing in Norway. They knew I had planned to call. That was the end of a very busy day. I looked out of my window and the Eiffel Tower was brilliantly lit up in all its glory. The city of Paris was at my feet! Yes, I slept well that night. That is, what was left of it!

The next day I was up bright and early. I had a nice breakfast in the hotel. It was a cheery restaurant with beautiful stained glass windows. I didn't feel alone even though I was alone. Then off I went to find my tour of the day.

I looked over the brochures and made my decision to go to Giverny, where the painter Monet's home was located. I had painted a number of good oils myself. I had made some lovely copies of his work. The day was beautiful. It was a perfect day to see the painter's home and gardens. I was happy to get on the bus and get on my way.

We arrived at Giverny. It was a painter's paradise. The house was a lovely shade of pink. The garden was filled with flowers of all kinds. The roses were beautiful around a trellis. Also the famous bridges, over man-made streams, that Monet had his landscapers construct for him, were lovely. The beauty of the house and garden, was a painting in itself.

Inside the house, Monet used bright primary colors. The kitchen was a cheerful bright yellow. Also the other rooms were colorful. I like color. I had made a good choice to spend the day there. I had taken a full roll of film, then the bus took us back to Paris.

For the second day of touring, I decided on a ticket to the Folies Bergere. It included a boat ride down the Seine, and dinner. Again it was a good choice. We traveled down the Seine through the City of Lights, another name for Paris. We went under bridges and saw glorious buildings. We saw a small replica of the Statue of Liberty on the banks of the Seine. I met a married couple from Canada. It might interest you to know that at no time did I feel an urgent need to use that French that I had learned from Madame Christian. Even the couple from Canada were delighted to speak English. The trip down the Seine, however, made me feel like a Parisian!

That evening our tour went to the Folies Bergere. It is the oldest Music Hall in Paris. It was immortalized in a painting by Monet. Charlie Chaplin, Josephine Baker, and Maurice Chevalier have been on its stage. In the lobby it was similar to the Moulin Rouge except that it was decorated with carousel horses that were beautifully placed around the room. Before the review started we were given a buffet of wine and cheese. The program was entertaining and colorful. I also liked the happy music! After the show we were taken to a Parisian bistro for the famous French onion soup. It was a good way to enjoy an "Evening in Paris!"

My third and last day in Paris. What to do? My decision was to go to Chartres. This was an elegant medieval cathedral. It was famous for its stained glass window. I would like that. It was another lovely summer day and I found the cathedral beautiful. Another plus for my very first solo trip abroad.

Now another night and the last night, what would it be? I decided to go on the tour titled, "Illuminations and Lido Show". This was a motorcoach tour of the illuminated sights and floodlit monuments of Paris. After that we were taken to a performance at the Lido. It was very similar to the Moulin Rouge and the Folies Bergere. We were then taken back to our hotel.

I was up early to take leave of Paris. This was the day that I would take the Orient Express to London. It was a moment long awaited. I arrived at the grand train station in Paris. I looked at the Arrival and Departure sign. I saw that the Orient Express was departing at ten o'clock. When the train arrived, a red carpet was placed appropriately for the new passengers to be able to walk to it in style. I was happily smiling as a porter carried my one small bag on to the train. I was then ushered to a private room on a coach. Oh, how pretty! There was a soft couch with white lace doilies on the arms and back. There was a pink fringed lamp on a table by the window. There were some magazines strategically placed. A private restroom! Oh, my! No Agatha Christie murder here! The night I spent on this Orient Express was uneventful. I had dinner in a first class dining room. The train, however, left a lot to be desired as far as smooth riding went. I mentioned this to a passing conductor. He said that the engineer was not a Frenchman and that he was unfamiliar with the terrain!

In the morning when I went for what I hoped would be a nutritious breakfast that would last a while, that is not exactly what I found. On every plate was a lobster. This was supposedly a complimentary gourmet delicacy for the passengers. I asked that mine be taken away! My fare was fruit juice, cereal, eggs and a pancake "to splurge!" When the train arrived in Calais, we were transferred to a Channel ferry. This took us to England.

Once in the port in England, I boarded a train to London. I arrived at Victoria Station. A taxi took me to the Royal Lancaster hotel. A doorman with a high silk hat greeted me at the door. In the lobby were a number of wealthy Arabs dressed in their long white gowns and special head coverings. I was impressed!

My room was a delight to behold. I had a television, a double bed and a lovely bath, with a hair dryer. On the dresser was a bowl of fresh fruit and a menu with any meal I might want. It was heavenly but late in the day, so I opted to look at the television, and order a full course dinner! Also, from my window, I could see it had started to shower. I would be snug and warm for the night. Since family friends who lived in the London suburbs were expecting me to arrive, I gave them a call to tell them I had arrived safely. Then I settled down to enjoy some of the fruits of my travels thus far!

The next day, my relatives from the Mill Hill area of London came to visit. We had dinner in the main restaurant, which was called the Rose Room. There we had a pleasant reunion. The next day I toured London and saw the main sights of the city. Later in the day my relatives came for me and drove me to their house for dinner. I felt very much at home. My solo trip seemed to make sense. I did have friends on the other side of the Atlantic, in England. Time went quickly. There was so much to see and do with people that I knew. It was not long – three days to be exact – before I was preparing to return to the *QE2*. This time I did not have to catch a train. I was driven by Pat, with his wife Florrie and his children, to Southampton. It was a Sunday so it made a great outing for the family. Also they were looking forward to seeing the great ocean liner England had in its Cunard fleet!

Pat made the drive as pleasant as possible as we drove down the motorway to Southampton. We stopped at an English tearoom to chat and say our goodbyes. Then the big moment arrived. We could see the imposing sight of the *QE2* in the distance. Pat carried my blue bag up to the entrance pier. I showed my ticket and kissed everyone goodbye. Alas, I was on my own again and going home!

It was a good feeling to be back on the ship. It was nice to see friends again. I met a table companion who had gone on a cruise on the *QE2*. This was fantastic! Now I knew that if I made another trip, I would be able to remain aboard and stop at ports in other countries. The ship was becoming an obsession with me. This was the way to go!

On this return trip, I decided to buy an evening gown, regardless of the price. I would give myself a little glitter and look as though I really belonged. With that future objective in mind, I went to look for my cabin. It was another single cabin with a porthole. I put my bag in my room along with the straw cowboy hat that the French motorcyclists had given to me. They had given it to me because they would no longer need it racing around France on a motorcycle! I had accepted it as a momento of the French experience. I had at least made a couple of friends!

I bought a long black dress with black sequins. It was a modest, classic dress. I wore it to the first formal of the return crossing. The dress seemed to attract a share of attention. It made me feel assured of myself as a traveler. Now I would go home to relish the success!

Oh, yes, I did have one opportunity to use my French aboard ship. I sang *La Vie En Rose* in French in the Yacht Club. After all, life, for me, was truly in the pink!

Chapter Two
Iberian Cruise 1986

The year following that memorable first transatlantic voyage was another busy, busy year full of the usual activities. I continued wrapping yarn around myself, my brother's favorite quote. In the area of music, I continued playing the piano. I had the very best teacher, who had a Master's Degree in music, from New York University. As usual, in June, I was in a recital. However, my primary interest was singing. My vocal teacher's suggestion was that I sing some Italian arias. I was given an "Anthology of Twenty-Four Italian Songs and Arias". She liked this area of singing for me and I liked it as well. So it was that my interest in opera singing began to develop. Also, since the last *QE2* trip, I had developed an interest in further travel. I began planning for this summer of 1986.

I decided to take the Iberian Cruise. I left New York on 3rd August. I had learned about this cruise on last year's trip. I was ready to find out about it. It, no doubt, would be easier for a solo traveler than my last trip. I arrived at the pier in New York with a language teacher friend, Larry, who I had known since teaching in the same school system. He wanted to see me off on a bon voyage! I was wearing a gray skirt, white blouse and a pink casual jacket. I was feeling much happier than on the first trip because I knew I was to find old friends aboard. Also I would be sure to make new friends.

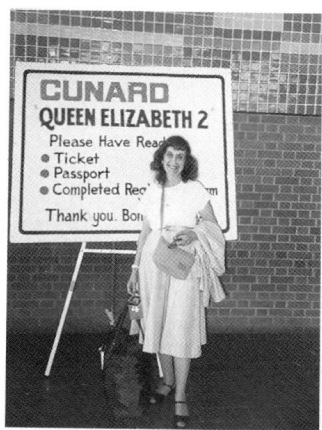

Leaving for the great solo voyage with ticket in hand and one bag – 1985.

Meeting Elaine Mackay, Social Directress, who allayed my fears.

Finding the first of eight pianos aboard.

Ready to sing *La Vie En Rose* in French. My signature song!

Arriving in Paris to take this picture! I really made it.

Boarding the Orient Express for London three days later.

Love to Florrie and Pat and daughter Elenora from the author.

A thrill to hear Big Ben chime at twelve noon.

Captain Lawrence Portet was the ship's captain. He was well-respected. The social directress was Elaine Mackay. It was always a pleasure to see her. She greeted me on this return trip with warmth. I would always look forward to her being aboard.

I went through the usual routine. I found my single room with a porthole. I found my life jacket and went through the usual fire drill practice. I then located the table that I would be seated at for the duration of the trip.

At my table were two very sophisticated ladies from Australia. They were very good company and much more worldly-wise than I. They were both married. The gowns they wore on formal nights were lower than low-cut. However, they were worn with such glamour that you accepted it as regular formal dress. I was wearing a summer cotton dress and I felt very comfy. I think they enjoyed my simplicity. Whatever, they were good company and years later we remained friends across the miles. Occasional calls from Australia were always a treat! Thank you, Ann!

Also seated at the table was a New York man who had a terrific appetite. He began his lunch and dinner with six glasses of Pepsi cola. I think he considered it an elixir of sorts. There were a few glances at this oddity, but he consumed them with such relish that no one said a word. The Pepsi marathon lasted throughout the trip. He also asked to finish anything that was left on the serving tray!

Wherever there was a piano, I would naturally see it. If there was a piano player seated at the piano, I was ready to listen. I'll tell you why.

My brother was an accomplished pianist. He had started with classical music and won many awards. Later, however, he became a pianist for a dance orchestra and he and his young friends played at the local dances. At home, he played the beautiful popular songs. He had a wonderful touch at the piano. This music I will never forget. He was my older brother and I was very proud of his talent. Consequently, alone and away on a super liner, I was glad to find a popular piano player friendly to me. Such was the case with Colin Brown. He played the classics very well and he also played popular music very well.

Colin played the piano for afternoon tea and every evening before dinner in the Double Down Aft Bar. On my schedule I circled the events that I would partake of for the day. I always had Colin's music hour on my list. On one such schedule I had listed all of the songs that he played. The list, you ask? *Where is Love, I'd Do Anything For Love, Moonlight Becomes You, The Summer Rose, A Nightingale Sang In Berkeley Square, Some Enchanted Evening, Younger Than Springtime Am I.* Colin had smiled to see me writing the names of the songs. Most of the passengers came to have an aperitif before dinner. I was just a smiling passenger who liked piano music very much. On this I concentrated.

The evening's entertainment was great, as is usual on the ship. The Peter Gordeno Show was exciting. He had some spectacular dances with his chorus, which he had choreographed. I enjoyed his shows. This trip, Richard Ianni sang at the ten o'clock shows in the Double Down Room and everyone liked his renditions of a variety of songs.

I enjoyed my table companions from Australia. They were fun to be with. I enjoyed the captain's cocktail party to which I had worn a yellow cotton dress. I enjoyed the evening, and I sang *La Vie En Rose* accompanied by Colin Brown. That evening I wore a rose-colored cotton dress. I had bought five such sleeveless dresses in as many colors as the store had, at the time! I bought a white, pink, yellow, rose and a flowered one. That was a spending spree! I loved the dresses and still like them! Now it was time to prepare for our arrival in Southampton.

The arrival in Southampton was an exciting moment. I looked forward to seeing the sail boats and preparing to disembark. Between three and four o'clock in the afternoon, we were cleared to go ashore. There was the *QE2* orchestra of Mick Urry and a champagne reception to toast our arrival in England. It was a happy moment for one and all. It was also a sad time to leave some of the good friends we had met. For me, on getting to the pier, I looked to see if I would see Elizabeth Taylor, the pier lady, as I called her. Then I proceeded to the buses that would take the Iberian passengers to the hotel where we were to spend the night. The *QE2* would be preparing for its new passengers the next day.

It was our turn to disembark. I looked about for Elizabeth Taylor, not really expecting to see her. However, there she was! We recognized each other immediately. It had been exactly a year ago that we had met at Southampton pier. Then she had escorted the travelers to Portsmouth to catch the ferry to Le Havre. We exchanged greetings and I took a picture. Then, on I went. Since there was a lapse of time before the ship would go on the Iberian cruise, we were given a complimentary night at the Polygon Trusthouse Forte hotel. We were also given a complimentary dinner and full breakfast. I was delighted!

When we arrived in the city of Southampton, it was early enough to take a walk around the town. Occasionally I met with other *QE2* travelers. Since this was my first chance to look about the city, I enjoyed it very much. However, it was the evening that impressed me the most. When dark settled over the town, I was snug and safe in my room, #228. However, that didn't keep me from looking out of my hotel window. It was a soft, quiet time in the city, and some people were leisurely walking about. There was a full moon! Close by was a clock tower. The clock tower was well lit and it was easy to see the time. All four sides had the time. As I looked, the clock struck ten o'clock with a sound much like that of Big Ben in London! I felt like a world traveler caught up in time in a Charles Dickens' novel. It was a scene that I would long remember!

On Saturday the 9th of August we were collected from the hotel and taken on a tour of Salisbury via Romsey and Stonehenge with a visit to Salisbury Cathedral including the viewing of the Magna Carta. Luncheon was also included in the tour before returning to the *QE2* via Winchester! This was all courtesy of the Cunard Line.

The *QE2* left Southampton at about 7 p.m. Commodore TD Ridley, RD, RNR, was at the helm. We were leaving for the Iberian ports of call which were Malaga, Gibraltar and Lisbon. We would spend a day in each port. Also, we had a choice of tours to various nearby places of interest in each port.

On passage to Malaga we were seated at the same table that we had had for the transatlantic crossing. The interesting Australian ladies were there, plus a refined journalist and his wife from Tokyo. The man was president of a local newspaper there. Also, there was a gentleman from Wimbledon, England. He owned a second home in the suburbs of Malaga, which he visited from time to time. He liked a lot of pepper on his food. So he was dubbed "Dr Pepper"! He enjoyed the name. We got along famously. This makes a voyage memorable.

The weather on passage to Malaga was divine. I had a chance to put on my bathing suit and sunbathe on the deck. It was very relaxing. Finally we arrived at our destination and it was time to follow the red *QE2* umbrella guide to our tour bus. I was scheduled to go to Granada, I was very excited. The beautiful *Queen Elizabeth II* had taken me to a country I had always wanted to see. At Penn State University, my Spanish professor had always said that he hoped that we would someday be able to visit Spain. He then said that if we did get to go we should make it a requirement that we visit the Alhambra. I was now looking forward to that moment. However, our trip there would be equally interesting. I remember the palm trees, the rolling hills, the beautiful blue skies and the occasional sound of accordion music playing in a restaurant. We finally arrived at the Alhambra. We all lined up at the entrance, waiting for our turn to enter. Apparently there were very many, many others with a similar goal in life. It was a hot, dry day and we waited impatiently! The Alhambra was certainly worth the wait. This remarkable shrine had been built by Moors after one of their invasions. I enjoyed the historical background. The mosaic, the arched scenic windows, the fabulous gardens, the fountains, were all so beautiful they were inspiring. Thank you, *QE2*, for taking me there! I made it, Professor!

For lunch that day we were taken to a restaurant for a Spanish style meal. The food was good and freshly cooked. We enjoyed it. However, what was even better, was the music that was being provided. Three students from Tuna University came to serenade us. Oh, that music sounded good to my ears. It was their singing along with their instrumental playing that really made me feel as though I had truly arrived in Spain. The students sold cassettes of their music. I was ready to buy one. I like to have good tapes to play in my automobile when driving.

Our next port of call was Gibraltar. I was looking forward to going ashore on the famous rock because I had traveled near it years before with my parents. I remember how impressed I had been to see it one moonlit evening while aboard the ship *Michelangelo*. Now, I would be able to actually walk on that great rock. However, we received an announcement from the

Commodore TD Ridley at 8 p.m., the evening before coming into port. It stated that the ship had received communication from Gibraltar that there was a strike in the port which included pilots, tugs, taxies, etc. It was recommended by the Gibraltar agents that we abort the call as we would not be able to enter the port. After the communication we got in touch with our Portuguese agents and were granted permission to call at Pria da Rocha the next day. We expected to arrive at 10.00 hours and sail for Lisbon at 19.00 hours. The tour manager was to announce details of available tours.

We arrived at Pria da Rocha. I was wearing my bathing suit with shorts to be ready for the beach. After the short tour, I was determined to get into the ocean. The Algarve was just my cup of tea. It was beautiful. There were palm trees, white stucco houses with red clay roofs, gardens for picnicking that had tropical birds perched on the limbs of the trees. It was divine. The hotel had a swimming pool that seemed to extend over the sea. I had met a fellow from Ireland who was also making the tour. He offered to take me for some refreshments at a little store and he took pictures of me at various places. On the beach I met some college students. We chatted together. They spoke some English and I spoke some of my Penn State Spanish. Language mission accomplished! I had wanted to see Gibraltar, but this had been a great alternative! Yes, the best part, I was able to go into the ocean, the great Mediterranean, and have my picture taken as I gingerly walked in the water!

On board activities were going on for the passengers. One of the Australian ladies, Ann, decided to enter the masquerade fancy dress parade. She was dressed as a French girl from Provence. She wore a long dress with a checkered tablecloth as a shawl. She carried a basket that contained bottles of champagne. It was all good fun. She enjoyed the moment and I enjoyed getting the picture.

Our next port of call was Lisbon. On board we went to exchange our money for escudos. I thought I might need it to buy some linen. The Portuguese are famous for hand made tablecloths. I also made reservations for a tour.

We arrived at the dock in Lisbon. It might have been close to where Christopher Columbus also docked. There was an impressive monument to the discoveries strategically placed so that no one could miss seeing it.

My tour bus was going to Sintra, Cabo da Roca and Estoril. The tour began with a drive through the main streets of Lisbon to King Edward VII Park to visit the tropical fernery. It was a beautiful botanical garden. I am a flower lover. This visit pleased me very much. I took a lot of pictures there. Upon leaving, I spied a Portuguese lady selling beautiful linen tablecloths. This was my golden opportunity to buy a tablecloth with twelve matching napkins, for my brother's wife. She would surely like the gift because she always set lovely table settings for the family on holidays. So, happily, I bought a set. The Portuguese lady was so happy and so was I. With light feet and happy heart, I proceeded back to the tour bus. The parking lot that had only our bus parked in it when we arrived, was now full of buses of all sorts and sizes. Oh my! Which bus was mine? I felt my heart quicken. I had not looked carefully at the number of my bus. Where could it be? Was I destined to live the rest of my life in Portugal? I went in and out of those buses as if in a maze. Finally someone on the bus recognized me and called. Whoever you were, thank you. Was it the anxiety in my demeanor?

Our next stop on this Iberian tour was a visit to Sintra. This was a town of ancient palaces and stately homes. We went through the Royal Palace. I was surprised by the ceiling portion of the palace. It was geometrically shaped. Then it was sectioned off with many squares and triangles. In each of these was painted a black crow. I'm sure the black bird must have had some significance in their ancient lore. Outside, a Portuguese lady was selling home-made craft dolls. I bought one, not only as a souvenir, but also to see the smile on her face when she made the sale! We were given a short time to wander about and then we were served lunch.

We then set off again via the Monserrate Road to Cabo da Roca. I am never pleased with driving on steep mountainous roads. However, I made it with everyone else to the top of a rocky cliff. From there you had an awesome panoramic view of the rugged coast. It was an exciting moment. A small shop sold tourist items. I bought a small dish with the words "Cabo Da Roca, Portugal" on it. Others bought a scroll that indicated that they had made it successfully to the top of this highest point in Portugal.

We finally descended and returned along the coast to the "riviera" resort of Estoril. It was a gorgeous place to enjoy a summer vacation. The weather was perfect. The scenery was lovely. The palm trees and homes were a happy blend. The tile decor of some of the buildings and the fishing villages all made this a delight.

We returned to Lisbon and to the *QE2*. We were finally on passage to Southampton. It was nice to be able to spend the day with my friends on board once more. My favorite entertainment for the evening was, of course, to listen to Colin Brown. I made my usual list for my brother to play when I got back home. He would be sure, however, to know all of the songs on the list. *Now is the Hour, Autumn Leaves, Endearing Young Charms, Elizabethan Serenade.* I was not familiar with the last song. Colin came from Scotland and I believe that some of the songs were indigenous to his country.

I had wonderful evening meals with my table friends. We talked about our tours. I told them about almost missing my bus. I vowed to be more observant next time. Of course, there would be a next time. I was a confirmed passenger! Dinner was often concluded with a flaming dessert of a fruit sauce that was simply delicious. This was the life! Dr Pepper had gone to check on his Mediterranean home. He presented me with a rose, for no reason except that he felt in a happy mood. I don't always understand the English, but I know they are very kind and respectful.

Also aboard I met two ladies from Rio de Janeiro. I had always wanted to go there when I was studying Spanish, so I found the ladies interesting. Their main reason for being aboard was to gamble. They had the money to do so. They were sister-in-laws from their many marriages. One I can quote as saying that she had been married seven times! She had a room in the penthouse section of the *QE2*. I had the opportunity to see her room. She had wanted an apron that I had purchased for an elderly friend of mine. Actually, I did not part with the gift. Anyway, she had a room that had a number of full-sized windows. It was splendid! All around the room were bouquets of flowers.

"Oh, my," I said. "What beautiful flowers you have."

She responded, "Yes, the ship's florist shop sends them to me every day."

I then replied, "The ship's florist doesn't send me any!"

Her reply: "Darling, I paid 'ten tousand dollas' for this room!"

Well, since I was located on deck four, I had no reply.
Her sister-in-law did not lack money, either. They had separate rooms and they gambled every day. That was one reason why she had not been able to buy gifts. Apparently one of them was not as adept at gambling as the other. One evening she was in a state of restrained tears. She had lost three hundred dollars at the gambling table. However, to make matters worse, she had

been told by the croupier that she didn't know how to play. This was a grave insult! She brooded over this for some time. She accused the person of rudeness and wanted her fired or replaced. I couldn't understand her plight since gambling was a no-no in my Christian family!

Finally, after a day at sea, we returned to Southampton. As usual, we were given a complimentary tour into the country. We went to visit Lord Mountbatten's home. It was a delightful home filled with mementos of his past and pictures of the Royal family. The estate was impressive.

From there we went to Lyndhurst and Lymington. The weather was beautiful. I carried a new purse which I had purchased in Spain and I felt as though I was in seventh heaven! We had lunch in a charming English roadside manor house. The flowers there were beautiful and the garden furnishings made it look picture perfect. I sat by a wishing well that was filled to the brim with lovely golden yellow marigolds.

We finally came to the city that I was looking forward to seeing again. It was Lymington. I had visited that city with my brother and his wife, and I was looking forward to seeing it again. We had slept in the Stanwell House hotel, and I wanted to see it again for old times' sake. Also, my friend Elizabeth Taylor, the pier lady, said it was her home town. Well, we arrived. Our bus parked not far from the center of Lymington. I was able to walk around the town. It was easy to find the Stanwell House. It looked exactly the same. I went in and saw the same little curio cabinet with dolls in it that I had admired before. It was a nice place to reminisce for a moment. Afterwards, my feet hastily led me to a favorite place in Lymington. It is the quay, pronounced "key", as I found out on that last trip. It is a lovely place to be. There are what looks like hundreds of small boats. Each boat has its name printed on the side. I guess the boats are owned by the locals and some are from other countries. Whatever, it is a beautiful sight. The seagulls are continuously swooping down, and people in a festive mood are strolling with their children or seated on the benches at the piers. This is my idea of good living. I would go back to Lymington any day!

On our way back to the *QE2*, we stopped in a small English town to hear a concert being played by the local high school students. It was a fine way to end a perfect day!

From the daily schedule, near the end of the Iberian cruise, I became aware of a talent show. Since I had been seriously studying voice, I thought it might be interesting to attend and find out what kinds of performances might be presented. So I sat in the audience and watched. Naturally, I was interested in any vocal or piano presentations. It so happened that a lady, wearing a red gown, was introduced to sing. She sang a popular song with maturity and confidence. She was sure of herself. I could only observe and contemplate!

We arrived back in Southampton. Now some passengers would be leaving and new passengers would be getting aboard. Colin Brown left. He went to Scotland for a home visit. I was sent a memo informing me of a cabin change. This sometimes happens when you book a trip of many segments. It is a bit uncomfortable to re-pack and move, but the steward is always helpful. I was moving from room 4177 to 4150. There was no great distance involved which made it easy.

Now on board, one could go to the beauty salon. The cosmeticians all wore pretty pink uniforms. They advertised to the passengers with brochures and short programs on the daily schedule. I finally decided to have my hair expertly washed and set. After having my hair done, I noticed that they had a special on foot-care. Since I did swim whenever possible, I thought it might be nice to have the foot treatment that included polishing the toenails. In my daily life style, I never had time for such professional luxury. This would be a first. I was given a foot massage in warm water. Then after my feet were dried, she prepared to polish the toenails. After a prolonged decision about the color, she set about preparing my toes. To do this, she had to use little toe separators. How cute! The English are so ingenious. Of course, it is probably done in the USA, but it was the first time for me. When I left the Steiners beauty salon I felt happy and light-footed, ready to enjoy the evening.

Before going to the captain's party in the evening, there was time in the afternoon to attend one of the daily activities. That afternoon I chose to go to an arts and craft class held by Marjorie Suszczynski. A group of ladies also gathered at the appropriate time which happened to be 2.30 p.m. The craft for the class was to make silk flowers. Marjorie was an expert in creating silk flowers. She had a business in the States doing just that. I followed her directions, enjoying the relaxed atmosphere. I set about putting silk petals together to form a flower and then putting the flowers together to form a corsage. The corsage was then trimmed with lovely ribbon that was inscribed with the words *Queen Elizabeth II*. I was quite proud of the creation. I have the corsage to this day as a souvenir.

The evening was special. Captain Portet was having his cocktail party. He would be having his picture taken with the passengers. He also used this occasion to introduce his staff. I wore the new gown that I had bought on board. Since I had not taken much in my limited bag, I needed to buy extra glamour. Also the dress would be a reminder of the trip. The dress was an off-white satin and lace dress that was appropriate for the occasion. Along with the other passengers, I waited in line to be introduced to the Captain and have a picture taken as we shook hands. It was a routine at all cocktail parties. I had a pleasant evening wearing my new gown and met many friends and took a lot of pictures. It was a great social evening. We would all look forward to the next day in the photograph section where we would find our picture taken with Captain Portet!

At dinner that evening a ship's officer came to sit at our table. This gave our table an air of importance. A pilot and his wife and daughter also sat at my table. Also a travel agent and her husband. It was a good group. The pilot enjoyed talking to the navigator of a ship. He said he would like to change his position as pilot to a navigator on a ship. The travel agent was very interesting. She and her husband were from South Carolina in the States. They invited me to visit. Also, they offered to arrange any of my future trips through their agency. The single girl at our table wore a gown of red sequins. It was red sequins from head to toe. On the floor we saw a few red sequins that had dropped off. She was in a happy mood. She had an interest in one of the waiters who passed our table with more than normal regularity. She did get to attend a waiter's party that is provided for the service help on the ship.

My interest on board was the music. Very often there was a performance in the theater. That evening Francis Heilbut was performing at the piano. He was the concert pianist for the trip. He was playing Beethoven's monumental *Hammerklavier Sonata*. I had met him a couple of times at my practice sessions late at night. I practiced my favorite *Moonlight Sonata* by Beethoven. I had all twenty-two pages memorized and enjoyed playing it at any available time. Although I played in recitals, I was by no means of the professional standard of Mr Heilbut. I thoroughly enjoyed his talent. Hearing such wonderful music while traveling made the *QE2* special to me!

In the morning, aboard ship, it is great to participate in some form of exercise. I liked the aerobic classes. I brought my aerobic outfit with me and made good use of it. The "Golden

Door" classes were held on six deck, F stairway. Other than going there, I liked to jog about on the deck to keep fit and enjoy the wonderful sea air. On some occasions I would find a secluded spot and sing out to the sea!

Since this was the last portion of the Iberian cruise, the transatlantic voyage back home, I decided to send a telegram. I would send one to my teacher friend, Larry, who was taking a short cruise on the *SS Festival* while I was gone. He would be surprised to hear from me and I knew he would like it. On 18th August I alerted the radio room to send a 'ship to ship' radio telegram. Two days later, I received notice that the telegram had not been delivered because the party was not on board! However, what had happened was that the first name had not been correct. I had sent it to 'Larry', and they had radioed 'Mary'! At that point it was too late to contact my friend!

I am not a movie fan. Each day a couple of movies were shown. Since most movies are not to my liking, I didn't waste my time by going. However, there were times when I did find a gap in my schedule and found time to 'take in' a movie. A comedy would do if all else failed. One day I went to see *The Money Pit*. It was a comedy depicting the perils and pitfalls of home renovation. Since a relative of mine was renovating their home, I thought it might be a good movie to see. I found it entertaining. Then, to be at sea traveling and able to relax in a movie theater, made the world seem a wonderful place. So, if you are traveling, this is another joy of sea travel!

Also on board were scheduled complimentary dance classes. I have always been interested in dancing of all types. However, I preferred modern dance, ballet and tap. I also enjoyed ballroom dancing, but I was a bit reluctant to get in with a group to practice new dance steps. I decided to give it 'a go' as the British might say. I found it interesting!

Another activity aboard was the fancy dress masquerade competition. The social directress had a trunk full of construction paper, crêpe paper and other odds and ends. The children particularly enjoyed participating, along with many creative adults. I watched the entries as they went by. One child was seated in a cardboard box replica of the *QE2*. It was complete with a large orange smoke stack. His mother had probably helped him put it together. It was very effective! I surely clapped for him as I saw his bright eyes shining. Other entries came out and a good time was had by all. I have a picture of the cardboard boat, whoever you may be, ten years later!

My pastime aboard was to play the piano each night. I had no serious plan to play in the talent show of which I now had become aware. However, I do believe that it came to me that perhaps I should sing one of the Italian arias that I had been singing during the year with my vocal teacher. The short song was titled *Nel Cor Pui Non Mi Sento* by Paisiello. I hardly remember the particulars, but somehow I did decide to enter.

In the afternoon I must have prepared. I know that I have a picture of myself at the microphone. I recall singing and having a shaky feeling in my legs because of performing on such a magnificent ship. So be it. I sang my song and received applause. Then I received a small *QE2* medal keepsake. To this day I can't recall anything significant except that the well-poised lady who had sung a popular song on the last trip, sang again at the end of this program. It happened to be at the time when preparations were being made for teatime! It was not a good time for her to perform. However, she came over to me and said she had enjoyed my singing. Then she asked the key of my little aria. I have a soprano voice that is in a high key category. I was pleased that she had come to compliment me. So, my love of singing on the *QE2* began.

The trip was coming to a close. Now we would begin packing to disembark. For the passengers' convenience, the US immigration officials were aboard. We were required to present our passport and a landing card. When this was done, we would need to wait until our deck was called. Of course, the night before all baggage was put outside our cabins to be taken to the pier.

In the morning I looked out at the familiar New York skyline. It was good to get back home. It was good to see the Statue of Liberty. When I walked down the gangway I had the normal bit of anxiety. Would my luggage be there? It was there, but it is always a tense moment. I had just two bags. I then looked for my limousine. The driver was to hold up my name on a card. It was another tense moment.

However, on this occasion, he was there. I had completed my second voyage on the *QE2*!

Chapter Three
Lisbon, Gibraltar, Pria da Rocha 1987

"Welcome Aboard! Captain Alan Bennell and his ship's company are delighted to welcome all who joined us today on board *Queen Elizabeth II.*" Then he went on to say that he hoped it would be a relaxing and exciting experience crossing the Atlantic on the ship's 620th voyage. Departing New York on Wednesday 15th July and arriving in Southampton at 5 p.m. on Monday 20th July, weather permitting. The year was 1987. Another year had gone by and once again I was aboard my favorite ship. It was surely getting to be a habit with me.

The year had literally rushed by. I was always knee deep in work and activities. My main calling was the singing. I kept studying my basics, such as breathing properly, yawning, for a relaxed position, and learning to purr! Along with these exercises, I continued to learn new ariettas. I learned *Caro Mio Ben* by Giordani, *Nina* by Pergolesa, and *O Cessate di Piagami* by Scarlatti. The more I learned the more I loved singing. I have a good memory. I was never challenged into remembering, I was so interested in the story that the words told, that I enjoyed relating the story in song even though it was in Italian. Italian was a language I had to learn. Consequently, language lessons were also a part of my busy schedule. Fortunately, a teacher friend, Larry, was a teacher of languages. I attended his classes and made good progress!

My piano lessons were by no means overlooked. They were an integral part of my day. My parents had started me on that instrument at a very young age. My older brother was a talented musician. So piano playing will always be part of my life. This year besides the usual practice materials, I concentrated on *Nocturne in E Flat*, by Chopin. I was also working on *Clair de Lune* by Claude Debussy and the *Sonata in C sharp minor, Op. 27, No. 2* known as the *Moonlight Sonata*. This year I performed the *Nocturne in E Flat*.

I arrived at the pier in New York wearing a summer white suit. I was beginning to look more like a controlled traveler. I would again look for friends aboard. Sure enough, Elaine Mackay, the social directress was there. The ship sailed at 6.30 p.m. The gangways were raised and the *Queen Elizabeth* started on its voyage of 3,158 nautical miles across the Atlantic Ocean. No matter how many sea voyages you may have taken, this is always an exciting moment.

I went through the usual procedure. I found my cabin, put down the carry-on luggage and prepared to take my usual walk about the ship. After all, it had been a whole year since my last sailing. This year the ship had undergone some refitting. I would find out what had changed. I walked up to the Queen's Room where I could hear music. I looked in. Before I could do much thinking on the subject, I was being asked to dance. I was not really interested at that moment because I had just said goodbye to my teacher friend Larry and I was feeling a bit misty. These big trips scared me a bit! However, I did dance with the nice gentleman. After one dance, I excused myself to continue my tour of the ship.

This year there were a number of changes. I know there had been some new parts put into the operating portion of the ship's engine room. However, there were some changes a passenger would notice. The changes were, number one, the spiral staircase in the Double Down room had been taken away. These stairs had given easy access to the mezzanine shopping level. We as passengers made use of this staircase, so I missed it! They had also changed an artistic feature of the ship that I had liked very much. It was the dance floor in the Lido. The dance floor had previously been covered with little colored lights that showed through the translucent floor. I had always admired that floor. Now it was gone!

We were assigned our table. The people were all congenial, but I must admit that by now I don't recall who they were. Also I began eating lunch in the Lido. It was a little faster and I could select my menu. It was here that I met Pamela Blake. She had been a stand in for a New York show called *Evita*. We both came from New Jersey, so we had a lot to talk about. Later on the trip she was billed as singer for the evening's entertainment. So being in the Lido for lunch one could see other travelers besides those at your assigned table.

The pianist aboard was an Arlene Daniels. Although my favorite pianist was not on board this trip, I did enjoy hearing the selection of songs that she played and also sang. Some of the songs that I listed were: *These Foolish Things Remind Me Of You, My Secret Love, I'm Feeling Like Someone In Love, I'll Take Romance, Till There Was You, Call Me Irresponsible,* and *The More I See You.* I would give my list to my brother when I returned home. That was one of his gifts. He would sit at the piano and play them for me.

On formal evenings we had an opportunity to have our picture taken with the captain. For this voyage, it happened to be Captain Bennell. He was a kind person who made everyone feel comfortable in his presence. He graciously allowed me to have a front view type of picture rather than the usual handshake picture. Everyone on board felt him to be a gracious person.

Since I am writing this book without any daily diary of my trip, I must rely on bits and pieces that are sometimes recalled in photos. One such experience was that of a singer of the evening. His name was Tony Monopoly. He was from Australia. He sang very well. The daily program indicated that he was an international singing star. I had not heard of him in the States. However, he asked all single ladies to raise their hands. I, of course, did so. Then he looked about and asked me to come on stage so that he could sing a song to me. I am naturally a very shy person, but the moment seemed to call me forward. I walked on stage in my pretty white dress and thoroughly enjoyed being sung to. It was a pleasant memory. There were many other such nice memories on the *QE2*.

It was once more that time when we would have to produce our passports before the landing procedure. I was off the ship in record time. I had a mission. Would I see the pier lady, Elizabeth Taylor? Without much looking, there she was! We exhibited our surprise. We had now met three summers running. I took a picture of her to record the moment. She was wearing her usual uniform of black suit, black tie, and black stockings. Now that that episode was over, I proceeded to look for my tour bus. For this, we followed the red *QE2* umbrella to our bus that would take us for a lovely ride through the New Forest.

There is nothing more relaxing than a slow drive through the New Forest on a beautiful sunny summer day. I was glad to be on "holiday" as the English call a vacation. The quiet, bucolic scenery was punctuated by quaint English cottages. Also there were green fields on which roamed beautiful horses. Horse owners are required to have a permit for each horse that grazes in the New Forest. Also there was an occasional inn. We stopped at the Lamb Inn. There we had some morning refreshments. It was a pleasant rest stop before continuing on to other sights in the New Forest.

We were back on the ship. Now we would meet new people who boarded in Southampton. I call this the British contingency. Most of the new passengers were from England. I liked this very much because I was fond of the English and most everything English.

The ship continued its cruise. It was a short day's voyage to get to Lisbon. I seem to be fascinated by the city of Lisbon. As you have read, I had been there the year before. This year I reserved a tour of the new and old portions of the city. Lisbon itself is attractive. It has lovely open tiled city centers with imposing statues of their heroes. Also, there is an impressive bridge that spans the River Tagus and separates the new portion of the city from the old. We toured by bus, but we also had time to walk around to look about and make purchases. It was a lovely day and I found it enjoyable. Then we were taken over the bridge to the old city at the extremity of the bridge. There we saw a towering monument in modernistic, tall, straight lines with an opening in the center in which there was a cross! It was topped with a statue of Christ with outstretched arms. It was a most impressive sight. I likened it to the statue of Christ on top of Sugar Loaf Mountain in Brazil.

In the old city we were taken down some quaint streets that had balconies displaying the day's laundry. We also visited the beautiful tropical fernery that I had enjoyed so much on the last trip. It was lovely. There were many varieties of azaleas, roses, marigolds, carnations, fuchsias, etc. The beauty was also in the idealist little lakes with swans swimming about. I am very much an idealist and romantic. This was a setting that made me feel at peace. The gardens had a straw shade overhead instead of the usual glass. This kind of covering was said to allow more air to circulate. The light from it created a golden glow. I sat a while and admired. Remember, this was where I couldn't find my bus on the last trip. This time I had no trouble whatsoever!

As part of the Lisbon tour, we were taken to a wine cellar for a wine-tasting party. The Portuguese are famous for their wines. The grapes for it thrive in the warm and moist environment of the country. We were each given a glass of the local wine to sample. Each time a city is revisited we find something new that is of interest.

The following day we went to the Rock of Gibraltar. I had missed getting on the Rock on the previous year's trip, so, I was pleased to finally set foot on the famous landmark. The incentive to be on Gibraltar this trip was to see the very special local apes indigenous only to his island. We were escorted to the top of the rock. There, lo and behold, were the apes. They were precious. The families of mother and babies were so appealing! It was well worth the trip so see the playful young apes. Back down from the mountain of the apes we were on ground level ready to enter the caves. It was said that the caves extended underground to the mainland. It was thought that in some previous era the Barbary Apes had come through the caves to settle on the rock. I am not fond of caves. I was glad when that part of the tour was over and we were back to the sunny, pleasant surface. There we were allowed to visit the colorful markets resplendent with bright umbrellas. It was there that I bought a small ceramic Barbary Ape with the word "Gibraltar" carved on it. I also bought a cuddly soft ape for the children in the family. I also bought a tee-shirt designed with a palm tree and a Barbary Ape hanging from it, and some green sequins liberally sprinkled about on the swinging ape's eyes and on the palm trees! I was ready to show the world that I had been to the Rock of Gibraltar! I have worn the shirt only once and that was to the cocktail party on the ship the following night. It was thoroughly enjoyed by everyone there who had been wise enough to reject it outright at the market... seasoned travelers, I presume!

We were back on the *QE2*. Now we would be having a sea voyage back to Southampton. It so happened that something happened to one of the ship's engines. We were stalled. We needed to wait until a part was replaced. That would come from Germany where the refitting had taken place. They would fly the piece over by helicopter. Before I had left on this particular trip, my brother had said that if an engine goes out on a ship, it simply stays afloat. It just doesn't go anywhere. It was with this bit of information that I accepted the situation without a feeling of fear. Our entertainment on board continued as usual. Since we would be arriving late, some travelers were changing their reservation dates for planes and hotels. Other than that all went along as usual. The sea was a lovely blue, and calm. We had a fine time to sunbathe on deck. Also at this time I know that I made a ship to shore radio phone call from the mid Mediterranean where we were waiting for the turbo engine part. The call was made home to the United States for $74.23. I didn't mind because I thought my brother's family might have heard about our delay! Anyway it was always a thrill for me to call home.

During free moments, I enjoyed playing the Steinway outside the Midshipman's Bar. At that time I was playing *Clair de Lune* by Debussy as part of my repertoire. I also had been vocalizing to an aria called *O Mio Babbino Caro* by Puccini. I had fallen in love with the aria when I had heard it sung at the beginning of the English movie *A Room with a View*. My singing coach and I went over every inch of the piece. The more I sang it the more she approved. It still remains a favorite of mine.

It happened that a pianist by the name of Brooks Aehron was performing for the cruise. He had a unique kind of artistry. I recall him playing the piano in typewriter fashion. The audience enjoyed that very much. He also played some more serious piano compositions, one of which was in my repertoire. It was the *Clair de Lune* that I mentioned before. I was pleased to watch him play that composition with such grace and feeling. I can easily recall the activities and entertainers aboard because I kept all of the daily schedules. I kept the schedules because my trips on the *QE2* were so enjoyable, having spent time just teaching! I had no intention of writing a book about these wonderful experiences. Now, it seems appropriate to do so with you the traveler and reader to recall the travels and have you travel along with me on this gracious ship!

We had a varied choice of daily activities. Some of the choices were: morning jogging classes, brain teasers at the library, bridge lessons, computer seminars, interviews with prominent personalities of the time, golf, lectures on various subjects, movies in the afternoon and evenings, crafts, and when all else fails, there's bingo! Everyone could choose whatever they liked. To compliment the activities were meal times, plus teatime and the evening buffet!

We finally arrived back in Southampton. It is always a pleasure to see the sailboats there to greet us on a lovely summer blue-sky day. Many of the passengers who were disembarking were making revisions to their landing schedules that, of course, had been delayed by a day! Those remaining for onward travel to New York were given a complimentary tour.

Our tour this year was to the beautiful New Forest again. We were also taken to Stonehenge. It is a treat to be on a bus after traveling at sea. We saw the horses grazing. We saw the English cottages with their thatched roofs. Finally we arrived at Stonehenge. This amazing grouping of huge stone slabs is arranged in a circle. Supposedly it was an instrument connected to the time or seasons that could be told by recognizing shadows at various times of the day and seasons. These rocks were arranged by the Druids before the birth of Christ. Later on, during the tour we were taken to the Forest Point hotel and restaurant for lunch. It was a charming place and we enjoyed the lunch.

We were back aboard the *QE2* for the transatlantic voyage. At this point, it would be my sixth transatlantic voyage. I now upgraded myself to eating in the Columbia restaurant! It is a lovely restaurant. As one walks in, you see a display table. In the center of the table, encased in glass, is a sterling silver loving cup. It stands at least two feet tall and is embossed with designs. There is a plaque at the bottom that stated that the cup was awarded to the Cunard Line during its early transatlantic voyages. It was given by the city of Boston, Massachusetts. The interesting fact about this beautiful cup was that it had been stolen. It was not retrieved until twenty years later! It was then returned to the Cunard Line. Now, it is encased in glass and it was at the entrance table of the Columbia restaurant. The cup is such a wonderful work of art to see that henceforth, I ate only in the Columbia restaurant for my meals aboard ship!

My table companions on this return trip numbered eight. One place was set for a staff member. It was always a privilege to have an officer seated at your table. It was not often that we would have the pleasure of his company because he was a host at a table in another of the ship's restaurants. Whatever, we had a congenial table of people. Also, on special evenings a pianist with a string ensemble of musicians would come to play for us. It was then time for some dinner dancing. This was a nice element of the Columbia restaurant.

The captain for this portion of the trip was Captain Lawrence Portet. Apparently he was a well-liked Captain... unfortunately for all, he was retiring. This would be his last voyage. So, on Friday the 31st of July, 1987, a farewell dinner was held for the captain. It was a very special white-gloved affair. There were musicians and short acts to acclaim the special dinner in his honor. I was impressed and kept the menu among my souvenirs.

CAPTAIN'S FAREWELL DINNER

Hors d'oeuvres
Asparagus Wrapped in Parma Ham,
Served with Mayonnaise
Celery Salad,
Air-Dried Beef, Finely Garnished
Melon balls in Cointreau

Hot Hors d'oeuvres
Pasta with Baby Shrimps, Heavy Cream, Cognac and Parmesan Cheese

Soups
Clear Oxtail Soup with Old Sherry Served with Chester Sticks
Cream of Chicken Reine Margot
Banana Bowl with Papaya

Fish Dish
Dover Sole Meuniere Sautéed in Butter
Served with Carrots and Boiled New Potatoes

Sherbet
Orange Sherbet

Main Dishes
Roast American Prime Rib au jus
Served with Baked Potato with Sour Cream and Chives

Stuffed Escalope of Veal Cordon Bleu, fired in Butter and
Served with Parsley Potatoes and Caesar Salade Mode du Chef

Crispy Roast Duckling a L'Orange
Served with Grand Marnier Flavored Duck Sauce and
Glazed Chestnuts

Vegetables and Potatoes
Asparagus with Hollandaise Brussel Sprouts Red Cabbage
Baked Parsley Pommes Berny

Salads and Dressings
Boston, Tomato and Cucumber
French, Thousand Island, Rogefort, Italian

Desserts, Ice Cream & Dessert Sauces
Iced Grand Marnier Soufflé Bavarian Cream with Passion Fruit
Black Forest Gateau
Ice Cream: Vanilla, Creamsicle, Cafe Espresso
Dessert Sauces: Strawberry, Chocolate
Fresh Fruit in Season
Assorted Cheeses with Crackers

Freshly Brewed Decaffeinated Coffee, Coffee, Tea
Petit Fours

So you see what a gala dinner we had. Certainly it was not the kind of dinner I would normally get at home. Good luck to a great sea captain, Captain Portet!

Also on Friday the 31st was scheduled the passenger talent show. Since I had studied long and hard with my vocal lessons, I was prepared this time to give it a more serious try. I signed up for the show. Now I would have that chance to find out about relating to the public with my song. So this time I brought along the musical composition so that the pianist could follow it to accompany me. It wasn't easy, I was soon to find out. The aria I had chosen was the *O Mio Babbino Caro* by Puccini. Most of the musicians played popular music or did a great deal of improvisations. I was used to a classical accompanist. It required some rehearsing on both our parts to come up with a suitable rendition of the lovely aria.

On the special hour of the show I came wearing a casual knee-length dress. I faced the public with no qualms about my music, but the experience before the passengers of the *QE2* made me feel as though my legs were made of rubber. I kept telling myself that although I felt I had unsteady legs, no one would notice. What I did know was how to sing the beautiful aria! It went well as any talent show act might. However, I was to remember that feeling even though it apparently did not interfere with my song. Now I would go home satisfied that I had approached the challenge. Next time, if there was a next time, I would have had some experience!

The trip was coming to a close. We, the passengers, had been presented with the best in travel. It was time to pack our bags. That had to be done by midnight. This was always a challenge. I always wondered what to do with my sleep pajamas in the morning. I solved that by having a tote bag for the purpose of carrying any left over items. Memories of the happy days lingered as I put into the tote bag all of the film I had taken with my trusty Cameron Sure Shot camera. They would be the happy aftermath of the trip when I put them together in an album of the 1987 highlights!

Disembarkation was as exciting as embarkation. You needed to have your passport and landing card in hand. All passengers had to wait until their deck was called. It was a moment for me to wonder if my limousine would be available when I finally made my appearance. Also, looking for your particular bags among a sea of other similar bags was a major concern. On later trips I learned it was helpful if I put wide pink ribbons on my luggage. I was then able to identify them quickly and easily. The limousine driver was supposed to hold up a card with my name on it. However, often I would need to wait or even make a call to the main office. Then I was usually told that my car and driver were at the pier but that the driver was having difficulty getting close to the exit berth to pick up my baggage. Eventually, he arrived, and I was on my way out of New York and on toward New Jersey and home sweet home!

It was a great moment to get back home and tell my folks all of my exciting adventures. However, it wasn't long before I was back to my music lessons again. I had a report for my vocal coach. I gave her all the particulars of my singing of *O Mio Babbino Caro*. She was pleased. It occurred to me that it would have been nice if I had recorded the performance. So it was that I went around town to find a recorder that would be easy enough to carry on my travels. Surely, I would go on the *Queen Elizabeth II* again! This time, however, I would be prepared with a tape recorder to document my progress and go over the cassette with my teacher to make any improvement. I did buy the recorder and used it even to tape some vocal warm-ups that I was taught. It could also be used in my stateroom to warm up before singing in the talent show. So my recorder became another essential for trips, besides the camera!

Among the many new songs that I was vocalizing this year came another Puccini aria called *Quando Me'n Vo Soletta*. Translated it means "When I Walk Alone". In the opera *La Boheme*, the part is played by Muzette, who is the town flirt! In the aria she sings about her beauty and the attention that she attracts when she goes out walking. It is a happy and colorful part of the opera. My vocal teacher suggested that I sing it. That is, that I start by studying the vowel sounds and voice projection. Believe me, when I practice I put everything I have into it. I go over the proper pronunciations of the Italian words. I make sure I know the translated meaning. I also make it a point to see the opera wherever it is being performed. If I can't do that, I watch it on video. I become totally familiar with the piece. Therefore, I never lack knowledge of the words and melody of an aria that I learn.

Onward to another year of piano study of the classics. My teacher was a demanding instructor. I had scale study in every key imaginable, including Dorian and Oriental scales. I had practice study of composers that sounded off key and with no discernible melody at all, and duets that were not to my liking. Along with all of this I would have a piece that I was working on, part by part, until completely memorized. This I did with the twenty-two pages of Beethoven's *Moonlight Sonata*. This composition I dearly loved. There is no doubt that piano playing is definitely a part of my life. However, I was continually coming to the realization that I was becoming extremely interested in vocalizing in the classic arias.

I began to turn my attentions to the local Rutgers University School of Music. I was familiar with this university because I had worked toward a doctorate in philosophy there with Dr Wheeler, the head of the department at that time. Now, I found that my interests were a combination of both subjects. I had at home my father's philosophy books and his selections of music copies. He was a violinist. It was music, however, that really came forth as top priority of my life. To this world of music I hoped to continue along with traveling to interesting ports of call. How, you ask? On the *QE2*!

The year of 1987 passed with the mundane and the musical intertwined. It went along until the travel brochures for 1988 started arriving at my home. It was time to think about summer travel. I began to wonder if I would find an interesting cruise that was different from the last two that I had taken. I was going to be a seasoned traveler, so I thought. However, it was much too soon for that thought to enter my mind. I would just travel and enjoy. The transatlantic voyages were a sure thing: as you know by now, dear reader, I don't fancy air travel. I have traveled to Europe by plane and while it was pleasant, I never could get used to the airports. On all of the occasions that I have flown, I have experienced delays. On two occasions we had a five hour wait in New York and Shannon airports during a strike of airport personnel. At the end of the five hours the airport looked as if it had been blitzed. There were paper cups and lunch wrappings strewn about. When the 747 was ready, everyone gave a resounding cheer. Never again, thought I. I still receive Shannon airport tax deductible catalogues that I signed up for while waiting impatiently for the plane!

Now I would decide what trip I would reserve. The decision was to go to Norway. I was delighted! I had heard so much about the beautiful fjords of Norway and my sister-in-law's mother came from Sognefjord. Yes, my decision was made. It was Norway!

Chapter Four
Norwegian Fjord Cruise 1988

Wow! What a trip! This year was, as you know by now, 1988. As I look at my records I can tell this Norway cruise was full of interesting activities. I shall do my best to relay some of them to you on this armchair voyage of ours.

My first day aboard I went to have some tea. Teatime is always a nice relaxing time. I had completed my embarkation and was now ready to rest a bit. It so happened that a traveler seated not far from me introduced herself. She was a stunning-looking lady with light hair tinged with a bit of blonde. It was very attractive. Also she was wearing a white polka-dot dress and sporting large jeweled earrings and rings on her fingers. She was an impressive sight. That she wanted to talk piqued my interest. I mentioned that she had beautiful jewels. She then proceeded to show me more that she was carrying in her purse.

Wouldn't it be nice to have such jewels, I thought. I must buy a small blue ring similar to the huge one she was wearing. She came from Texas and was a beauty consultant of sorts and also a part-time travel agent. At this point, leaving from New York, she was my first acquaintance. We would meet again!

My table in the Columbia restaurant was a table for six. I have no recollection who the passengers were. I do know that one couple were on their honeymoon. They looked very happy and seemed to hold hands for the entire trip. I was my busy self, locating the pianos and practicing at every available moment. Also, at one point, I went to the hairdressers and asked that a bit of blonde color be washed into my hair. I had this done by having my long hair pulled through little holes in a rubber cap. It is a strange process, but I thought it might be worth it for a brighter look. It so happened that there was so little change, my brunette hair was just lightly brightened with a nice shine. It was pretty. I liked it and thought Steiners, the hairdressers aboard, did a nice, natural job.

Captain Alan Bennell was the captain of the ship for this transatlantic crossing. It was always comforting to travel aboard with a captain who I had been with on other voyages.

Also aboard was the concert pianist, Francis Heilbut. He would be performing in the theater. On stage there, they had their largest grand piano aboard. It was reserved for classical concerts. The evening of 11th July, he would play some of his classic repertoire. I looked forward to that. At the door our programs were given to us. I found out that he would be playing Beethoven's *Moonlight Sonata*. He played all three movements with great talent and expression. I later got to talk to him. I always had in mind the possibility that I would have a concert pianist accompany me when I sang. Now I had come aboard with my music and it would be a challenge to find just the right accompanist for the aria.

On previous trips I had managed to sing at least by the return Atlantic crossing. This trip I was ready on the first crossing over to England. I had my warm-up tape with me to get ready for the talent show. I wore, as usual, a summer cotton dress. This was a pretty light-pink dress. In my hair I wore a matching pink flower. To give my legs a steady feeling, I wore ballet slippers that I had worn in my ballet class at the YWCA. I felt very comfortable and casual holding a pair of small pink gloves. This was to give the appearance that I was out walking.

I would be ready to sing *Quando Me'n Vo Soletta*, from the opera *La Boheme*.

At the appropriate time I went up to the Grand Lounge. I had met the pianist who would accompany me. We had a brief chance to go over the aria together. It certainly was quickly done and by no means as accurate as it should be. However, the show must go on and I was ready. I had my camera in one hand, my recorder in the other and my small gold purse. Now let me see if I was making any improvement. I wanted very much to sing my heart out just as Muzette did in the opera.

To introduce the talents who were performing was a staff member by the name of Paul. I don't recall his last name. He was a personable individual who was always in a happy mood. When he came on stage, I noticed his British humor was in full swing. I do believe that it is .thought that these amateur performers would feel more relaxed with humorous introductions. He began his show with a snappy rendition of *There's No Business Like Show Business*. Then he said in an affable tone of voice, "Have we got a show for you, have we got a show for you?" At this point the audience laughed at his implication. I was finding out that there was nothing sacred about a talent show under his auspices. So be it! He went on in the same manner. It then came time for him to introduce me.

He began with "Our next artist (he pronounced it 'arteest'), is well known for her singing. If you have heard her before, you are in for a treat. If you haven't heard her sing, the doors are locked." Laughter, laughter! He went on, "She's from New Jersey and is going to sing for us." I had a section clapping for me. "I know fellows, she's good, but not that good!" He went on that I would sing *Going My Way* from *La Boheme*. "MARY MASTONY!"

After singing I received great applause. I happen to have the recording of it at this moment. It was quite nice. Next time I will have to put the recorder on a soft surface. This had picked up some of the motion of the ship because I had placed it on the small marble tea table. I concluded my singing with a round of applause from the audience, and a round of applause for the accompanist, whom Paul said was not used to playing classical accompaniments, but did very well on such short notice. I was given my very first red *QE2* umbrella. I wondered at the time what I would do with the umbrella since I was on the ship most of the time. However, I soon found out on my first tour of Norway. It came in very handy, I loved having it and also taking pictures using it. Yes, I became more and more of a *QE2* fan!

While I was interested in music, my new-found friend had other things in mind. She had recently divorced and was open to meeting people. It so happened that one evening we sat listening to the band playing some dance music.

She leaned over to me and said, "Do you see that good-looking man who just passed by?" I said yes, I had seen him, "Well," she went on, "his wife just passed away. I heard him talking about it to someone at the bar."

It wasn't long after that when he apparently saw her. He walked over to where we were seated and said, "I see the photographer is taking pictures. I don't want to take a picture alone. Would you be so kind as to have your picture taken with me?"

She looked festive in her beautiful gown, so she accepted the invitation. It became an on-board romance! He was from England and although she lived in Texas, she was born in Manchester, England. They made a nice couple and I was glad to play Cupid. I was rewarded one evening with one red rose from a bouquet that he was giving to her. I had always told her that I thought he was a very nice person and one in whom she might very well take an interest. I do believe that I was helpful to their new relationship. They eventually married about a year later. Congratulations again!

On board activities consisted of those that I had become used to. I did like the Elaine Mackay classes. She had one class about napkin folding. It was interesting. We made various shapes. She showed us how to make the hat shape, a pointed cone. She showed us how to make the fan shape. This I liked and very often use it at my dinner table. It is very easily made with a napkin folded in half and then folded in and out as for a fan. Then the ends support the fan as it stands. Try it. It's easy. I also liked one that she made for paper napkins. It was the butterfly. You fold a paper napkin into a triangle. Then you place the center part into the two prongs of a fork. Voila! You have a butterfly. If you use colored napkins, it is very effective for a summer table setting. Thank you, Elaine Mackay!

We finally arrived in Southampton. Those of us who were continuing on the cruise, were taken on a tour of the New Forest after arrival. I saw Elizabeth Taylor, the pier lady, busily attending to lines of people at the ticket counter. We exchanged greetings. Then I went on to see the New Forest and all of the wonderful horses and cottages. It is always relaxing for me to know that I have arrived in Great Britain and that I was am again in the New Forest! I passed a lovely country church. The blue colored identification board indicated it was "The Church of Saint Michael and All Angels" in the diocese of Winchester. I took particular note of this beautiful church because my brother's name is Michael, as in Michelangelo, to be exact. I thought he would enjoy seeing a picture of it. This time we were taken to the most picturesque of restaurants, in the New Forest, that I had ever been to with the tour. It was situated next to a lovely body of blue water. I don't know if it was a river or a lake. It did have a small sightseeing boat ready at the shoreline. I ate at an outdoor table in the lovely English sunshine. For some reason, the sun was always shining whenever I toured the New Forest!

By late afternoon we were back on the ship. On deck music was being played. Then later, before the gangplanks were raised, the city of Winchester brass band played us away.

We set sail for Norway and the fjords. The captain for the cruise was Captain Alan Bennell. We were on our way to Norway. It was really exciting. At my table for the cruise, I was fortunate to have Elaine Mackay, the social directress. There was also a Swede and a German. It was an interesting combination.

On board, with the other English people, came the comedian who would be entertaining us. He was an English TV personality. Apparently wherever he performed on the ship he had a huge following. One day I happened to be walking by as he was performing at the Midships Bar area. I had not seen the entertainer before, so I turned my head to look as I was walking by.

To my astonishment he called out, "You in the frock."

It was a surprise to hear my dress called a frock! However, I stopped. He then proceeded to say in front of his audience, "Come over here and dance with me."

The audience, of course, laughed because of his funny smile. I went forward, feeling immediately like part of the show. Soon I was whirling about. As we danced, I noticed that one of his rhythm band members had on two different types of shoes. This I was happy to bring to his attention. He then made some funny comment to the audience about the musician.

By this time, I had begun to understand the humor of this English comic and why he was so popular. He then asked me what number I would like to have the band play. I told him. I went on to sit and listen to their rendition of *Deep Purple*. I stayed for the rest of his show. Later, I found out his name was Jim Bowen.

I spent a lot of time on deck. I was anxious to see the fjords. I looked expectantly at every mountain that came into sight. The first Norwegian town that we came to was Flaam. The daily schedule had a picture of a Viking boat with the words "Beldommen Til Flaam"! When we arrived in Flaam, it was raining heavily. I was ready with my London fog raincoat and hat and my new red *QE2* umbrella that had been given to me at the talent show! I was accompanied by another lady who was also visiting Flaam. She helped by taking pictures of me under the red umbrella! The first point of interest was a statue of a man by the name of Christiansen. It happened to be the maiden name of my sister-in-law. I knew then that I was certainly in Norway. Then my eye caught a small cruise boat with a sign above it in large letters. It read, SOGNEFJORD CRUISE. My sister-in-law's mother came from Sognefjord. I was delighted. I would have these interesting pictures to show her when I arrived back home. There wasn't much more to see in Flaam. However, I was satisfied.

By late afternoon we were back on the ship. In the theater there was an informal lecture on the ports that we would enter at the next stops. On the agenda was Hellesylt, Geiranger and Bergen. A lecturer from Norway told us about the areas to be visited. Also that evening was the invitation from the captain to attend his cocktail party in the Queen's Room from 6.45 p.m. to 7.45 p.m. The captain would introduce his senior management team and would be delighted to meet his guests individually and be photographed with the passengers, if desired. The invitation was an alert to get out your formal wear. I had brought along a pink gown with little glittering rhinestone sprinkles about. It was a gown that I had worn to a wedding. I thought it would be a good one to be photographed in with the captain. The picture came out very well and the evening was pleasant as usual, with music, champagne and happy conversation.

Monday 18th of July 1988, voyage 667 #4, we came into the port of Alesund. There was a grand blue uniformed band that met us at the pier. Also girls in Norwegian costumes were nearby selling gift items. I stayed in the town to enjoy the local color and activities. There were lovely shopping centers with flower-bedecked malls. The weather was beautiful. Along the pier where the *QE2* was docked, was an enchanting quay. The small boats were a joy to see. I took a lot of happy pictures.

A rather remarkable event occurred that day aboard the ship. A beautiful multi-colored hot air balloon was assembled and made ready for take off. We were all on deck to witness the procedure. It was quite a sight to see as it took off from the deck. I have not seen such an event since. It helped to make the cruise even more exciting.

"Velkommen til Hellesylt and Geiranger" was the title on my daily schedule for Tuesday, 19th July, 1988. It then stated that in Norway skiing, jumping and cross country races stand among the strongest in the world. Here is the most tradition-steeped ski run in the world, having been organized every year since 1892. So you know the kind of country we were approaching. I could tell from the windows of the *QE2* that the mountain peaks outside were still covered with snow in the month of July.

The ship docked at Hellesylt to allow passengers to explore some of the mountainous parts of Norway by tours. These tours would eventually arrive at Geiranger. I opted to go directly to Geiranger, since mountains were always a source of apprehension to me. I had driven some high roads in the Sierras in California and also some of the Alps. Hairpin bends were just not my cup of tea!

At about 10 a.m. the *QE2* anchored in Geiranger Fjord. The gangways were located on five deck aft. I made my way there. I usually wore my London fog raincoat because sitting in the tender was often misty. However this day was so sunny and warm, I simply wore my white slacks outfit, a white visor cap and a white bag for souvenirs that I might buy.

Geiranger Fjord was so beautiful that I must say it was my favorite "R and R" stop. That is, "rest and relaxation" stop. I loved just walking about meeting *QE2* friends and shopping for Norwegian gifts. Many of the people strolling by were also residents of the area. They were out this sunny day buying ice cream and pushing strollers. Seagulls were flying overhead. A small piper cub plane was taking passengers for a once in a lifetime view of the spectacular fjords. I thoroughly enjoyed my day and was sorry to take the last launch back to our ship. I didn't know at the time that I would be returning to Geiranger in the future.

Back aboard, I decided to go on deck and get a suntan and enjoy the scenery of the fjords with their waterfalls on unexpected precipitous mountain sides. It was so peaceful. It felt indulgent of me to be in such serene surroundings. I never thought the summer days could be so warm and deliciously pleasant. We were served hot tea or a cool drink if we wished, as we sat reclining in our deck chairs. This was a bit of heaven!

In the evening we had entertainment, as usual, commencing with a gourmet dinner. This, plus traveling companions, and a visit at our table from an officer dressed in his white uniform was a great start to the evening. Later on in the evening there was a show in the Grand Lounge. It was called "Inspired by Fred Astaire". It was a show written and produced by Peter Gordeno and Jonathan Lesser starring the Peter Gordeno Dancers. They were always very exciting to watch. I do believe they were the best that I saw aboard ship. Their show was followed by *Putting on the Ritz*. The Steve and Debbie dance team with the Mick Urry Orchestra went back in time for us to enjoy the fabulous razzle dazzle of the 1930s. Thus the evenings were thoroughly entertaining.

The next port was Bergen. I was looking forward to going to Bergen because I was working on the first movement of Grieg's *Concerto in A Minor*. It would be inspiring to see Edvard Grieg's home which I knew was in Bergen, Norway. I reserved the tour that would take us around the environs of Bergen. Included in the tour was a visit to the composer's home.

"Velkommen Til Bergen." On Wednesday, 20th July 1988 we arrived in the port of Bergen. I selected the tour to Bergen, Trodhaugen and Fantoft. The bus left at 9 a.m. I arrived with some Norwegian kroners in my purse. It was always a temptation to bring home a souvenir as a remembrance. The ride on the bus was pleasant. It was interesting to see the Norwegian houses, so neat looking, in rows. It wasn't long before we arrived at Trodhaugen where Edvard Grieg's house was situated.

Our Norwegian guide was totally dressed in red. We had no chance of losing her on her continuous narrative about the home and the life of the composer. I kept no record of her narrative but I do remember some of the highlights. As one approached his home there was a small grass-roofed building that the guide told us was formerly for the servants but was now used as a souvenir shop. His own home was farther up on a hill. It was a rather modest two-story gray structure. The more interesting part was the interior of the home. On the walls were family portraits. Apparently his wife was a singer. There were pictures of her. He had composed works for singers. *Song of Norway* was presented as an operetta in San Francisco, California. In one corner of the room was his grand piano.

Edvard Grieg did most of his composing in a lake house that he had built at the bottom of the hill, next to the lake that was there. It was a lovely setting for composing. His music is so typical of the landscape of his native country. His music had the sound of open space with the flourish of waterfalls! It was here that he composed the wonderful *Concerto in A Minor* for which he was famous. He was friends with Franz Liszt. He often went to Liszt for advice. On one occasion he showed Franz his preliminary composition of the *Concerto*. Franz looked at the score and then sat down to play it perfectly and almost by heart. When he finished he enthusiastically assured Grieg that he had a great composition and that he surely should have it published. Thus the *Concerto in A Minor* was born! To me as a pianist, I found the story very interesting. Also to be at the lake and seeing the piano on which he composed, was certainly a privilege. Thank you, *QE2*, for coming here!

I would like to mention at this point, that I write this book as a conversation with the reader, whoever you may be. I suppose you have surmised as much. In general, most of the events are described as I recall them from years past, because it wasn't until now that I considered writing about these wonderful journeys on the *QE2*. So, dear reader, I hope you are finding our 'conversation' interesting.

Our tour traveled on to Fantoft. This part of the tour took us to see a stave church. Stave churches were the first churches built in Norway. There are few of them left today. Each one is prized for its historical value. The church in

Fantoft was lovely. It was completely constructed of wood, of which there is no shortage in Norway. I was told that even the adjoining links of the church were held together by a type of wooden nail. So the church was constructed entirely of wood! The interior art work was also typical of the earliest days of Christianity. Religious figures seemed to have no dimension. Since my visit, I read that one of the old stave churches had burned. It caused me to feel sad because I know how much the Norwegians treasured the churches.

Upon arriving back in Southampton I took the boat train to London. My hotel was the Grosvenor Victoria. It is a particular favorite of mine for a number of reasons. I had stayed there with my brother and his wife on our first trip to London. Also, the hotel is centrally located. It is so easy to get around London's landmarks without even taking transportation.

Relatives in Mill Hill, a suburb of London, came to visit me. We had a tour of the town and then they drove me to dinner in their home. It gave me a sense of belonging. Having friends and family does help "make the world go around".

My schedule included a highlight that had always been a dream of mine. It was to visit Scotland. So it was that a Frames tour was included in the itinerary. It helped also to know that a flower show was being held in Glasgow that year. Although the flower show was not included in the tour, somehow I would make my way there.

We met at the Frames bus station in London. Shortly thereafter we started our ride toward Edinburgh, Scotland. The bus driver was very competent in driving and telling us historical facts about the English towns that we drove through. I was particularly pleased to pass through the birthplace of the ancestors of General George Washington. He was the father of my country. We had learned about George Washington since we were children in grammar school. Thus my interest in seeing this birthplace.

We continued our trip until we arrived at a small town outside of Edinburgh called Portobello. There we had reserved lodgings for the duration of our stay there. It was such a pleasant experience that just the remembrance of it is a happy one. First of all we were given a day at leisure to just walk about the town. This was a real joy. I took it upon myself to walk down Princes Street. Solo, and on a beautiful blue sky day, with the feeling of arrival, to the place that I had always wished to see, made my steps light and almost musical in nature. Well, dear folks, and some of you may be the Scottish friends who I have since met, this is what happened. As I walked down Princes Street, looking up at the castles and occasional Scotsmen dressed in kilts, something unexplainable happened. I had, for once in my life an "out of body" experience. It could not have lasted more than a moment. However, during that time, I had no feeling of my feet touching the ground. I was completely at one with my surroundings. It was a fantastic feeling. I shall never forget it!

We were taken into Edinburgh Castle. It is an impressive sight. We looked and enjoyed every rampart of the castle. Then we were taken to the level where the tattoo was held. It was fascinating to hear about the elaborate ceremony of great tradition. As we left the castle, there was a Scotsman in a kilt, playing the bagpipes. I had come to Edinburgh with dreams and they had now been fulfilled!

Each day that we stayed in Portobello, we were taken to a nearby site of interest. We went to the lakes and to Stirling Castle. In the evening they provided dinner and some entertainment. One evening they had some kilted Scots do their famous sword dance. The swords are crossed on the dance floor and the dancers dexterously dance between the blades of the swords. It is most entertaining to watch!

Finally, while in Scotland there was time to go off on my own to Glasgow. There was a local bus station nearby and I took a bus from there to the city. There they had a spectacular display of all kinds of flowers. It was their flower show. The day was spent admiring the blossoms. There was also a little train that took visitors to all parts of the exhibits of floral displays. It was a day well spent. It would make my memory of Scotland forever pleasing!

Back again to my favorite city of cities - London! It is no trouble for me to get around London, for as I mentioned, the Grosvenor hotel, where I like to stay, is centrally located. My main objective was to have a date with Big Ben, the famous clock tower. I took a walk through London, looking in the shops, sometimes having film developed in Boots, and then finally arriving at the little park at the foot of Big Ben. There I sat for a short while and waited for the clock to strike the hour. It always reminded me of my first trip to London with my brother and his wife. At that time we had driven to Big Ben in the evening and sat in the park to listen for the clock to strike the hour of midnight. Great memories!

In London, my other favorite pastime was to catch a sightseeing bus. How wonderful to sit on the top deck and view the entire city, with camera in hand. Any day, at any time, it would please me to go back to London if only to get on one of their sightseeing buses. The glory of life!

Westminster Cathedral was also close enough to my hotel to walk there. It so happened on this particular trip, when I entered, that a wedding was about to take place. Therefore, I stayed to watch it. It was absolutely beautiful. The church was completely decorated. The choir was in position with heavenly music. The bride was resplendent in a gorgeous white trailing gown. The groom was handsome in his formal attire. They were a splendid couple. Although I had no idea who they were, I sent my thoughts of good wishes for their future!

That evening in London I met with friends from the *QE2* to attend the show *Phantom of the Opera* at Her Majesty's theater. It was a splendid show. Hearing the song *Think of Me*, I could not help but feel the emotion of the words: "think of me fondly when we say goodbye." I had spent many hours with my teacher preparing to sing that very song! It is my favorite rendition in the show besides the song *The Magic of the Night*, sung by the phantom. It was a great way to end my land tour!

The next day preparations were made to meet up with the *QE2* in Southampton. There, it would also be nice to be back once again with my friends. So, from London I went to Waterloo station to catch the boat train back to Southampton. It is always great to see the ship waiting at the dock for its transatlantic voyage. I was aboard and through all of the formalities to which I had now become accustomed. The return trip had some of the people from the Norwegian trip on board. One such person was a Swedish person. He was a tall blond gentleman who worked in the bar service department. I never was sure of his status. Also at the table was the German who had spent his vacation in Germany. He constantly had trouble reading the menu. One evening our waiter decided that he would get help in translating the menu. The waiter looked far and wide on the ship for a person who could do some translating for the German passenger. Finally, we saw our English waiter return with a man from the Caribbean. In a short time he translated everything on the menu for the German. The German passenger said it was the best German he had ever heard spoken. The Swede was beside himself with surprise! I have met the Swede on other sailings and he has never failed to remember the translating episode!

The return trip was more or less the same as in the past. The captain was Alan Bennell. The second evening out to sea we had formal night. At that time we, the passengers, were again invited to his cocktail party. It was always an evening that was special. It was also the evening we would have our pictures taken with the captain. Also, the photographer would come to our restaurant to take a group picture which we could treasure for posterity. Then later in the evening there was dancing. The social directress was sometimes in charge of the festivities at the dances. She would have a set of dancers spotlighted. If you happened to be caught in the spotlight you received a bottle of champagne. I won a bottle one evening. I probably saved it to take home to my brother!

A favorite of mine was to go to the midnight buffet. It still is a favorite of mine. Goodness knows, one is well-fed aboard ship! However, for me it was the glamour to be up at that hour of the night. It was just extra fun to have a cup of tea and a bit of fruit and cheese cracker before retiring!

As the return crossing began to draw to a close, there were lectures to attend and also movies. I went to see and hear an informal lecture titled "The Crown Jewels, An Extravaganza of Diamonds". It was presented by Brigadier Kenneth Mears. He was the Keeper of the Crown Jewels. I found the lecture to be very interesting. I have since received a book as a gift with beautiful pictures of the crown jewels. It is interesting to read and to look at for visiting guests.

All good things must come to an end and so, with the last days approaching, I did not sing in the talent show because I had done so on the first transatlantic crossing. Without much ado, I packed my things together and took leave of the *QE2* for the year 1988. There would be more to come, I was certain!

Now at home there was time to meet with my brother's family and share the presents and experiences of Norway with them. This was also a happy time!

As the year progressed I was again deeply involved with my usual activities. I was taking continuous piano study to increase my repertoire. There was Bartok, Gershwin and the second movement of Grieg's *Concerto in A Minor*. This besides constant review of other selections kept me very busy.

My singing kept progressing. It became necessary to develop on a more intense level. With this in mind, I began what became four years of study at Rutgers University School of Music. Here I was able to continue classes in piano, voice and dance. It would become my most fulfilling years of study. With my musical background, it was great to be a part of the university music studies. Thus my year was totally scheduled until my next summer trip on the *QE2*!

Chapter Five
Scandinavian Cruise 1989

QUEEN ELIZABETH II Sailing 23rd July, 1989.
Here I go, about to take that trip again. There is a popular song that begins that way. Well, here we go. The excitement is great and all is ready for the voyage!
The mission for this trip was well-planned in advance. The hard-earned mission was to sing for the passengers of the ship. This trip was going to be a time of confidence and presentation. After all, all those days of music involvement at Rutgers University should have produced some good results. For me, it was a great thrill to be singing. It should have been my life's calling, but other more academic fields needed to be established on my road of life. Now the approach was being tried and loved.
The ports of call for this vacation were, in general, Norwegian. They were Hellesylt, Geiranger, Trondheim and Stavanger. The other two cities that followed, I had not visited. They were Copenhagen, in Denmark, and Oslo. It would be a great trip!
There was the *QE2* in New York harbor. Oh, how splendid it looked in the warm morning sun. This morning I wore a white cotton dress that seemed to be appropriate for the embarkation. Ordinarily I wore a leisure suit or dress with a jacket. This trip the weather was so warm and pleasant, this outfit was more comfortable. Up the gangway I went with

passport in hand. There in the Midships Lobby, was the receiving line composed of Elaine Mackay, Lindsay Frost and other members of the crew. It was such a nice feeling to see friends!

Now, on board, it is always a treat to go on deck and just look. There before you is the New York skyline. On a beautiful day it is so very impressive. The camera in hand, I was spurred on to picture taking. No matter how many times you see the New York skyline it is always exciting. I stayed on deck to see the Statue of Liberty. After that view, the passengers settle down to their transatlantic voyage.

The captain for this voyage was Captain Alan Bennell. He and his ship's company were delighted to welcome all of us who joined the ship that day. He hoped it would be a relaxing holiday and an exciting experience. This would be the 707th voyage to Southampton. We would arrive on 28th July at 1 p.m.

As was usual, on the day following embarkation, the UK immigration inspection took place. We would meet according to our cabin deck number. There we presented our passports and received a landing card. Also, at some point, we would have a fire drill. Then with these formalities over, we proceeded to enjoy the trip.

For entertainment we had a celebrity on board. This trip it was Robert Vaughn, an Academy Award nominee and star of stage and television. He would personally introduce a showing of the film *Superman II*. Also later in the trip he would be interviewed. That same day, in the evening, the singers and dancers of the Jean Ann Ryan Production Company would present "An Evening with the Music of Andrew Lloyd Webber". The Rob Charles Orchestra was the accompanying orchestra.

By the third day aboard, we were already signing up for shore excursions. I had selected a tour of Trondheim, which included a visit to the Folk Museum. I also selected a tour of Copenhagen with a visit to the Moscow Circus that would be performing. At the same time as making tour selections, came the time to place one's name in the talent show, which was normally held at this time, the day before disembarkation.

Now after a year of study at Rutgers University School of Music, it was time to prove myself in front of my favorite audience. During the year my very capable music professor had carefully taken me through all vocal exercises necessary for beautiful vocalization. The basic aria of the year was *Caro Nome* by Giuseppe Verdi. It is a difficult aria, but extremely beautiful. It has become my dearest favorite. At this time, it would be my first presentation. It would be very exciting. However, I was also learning to be relaxed. For the show, I wore an ankle length dress made of a soft lightweight cotton material. It had a soft drop shoulder treatment. It had a soft, light lavender, floral design. With the dress I wore black ballet slippers that tied at the ankles. They were very comfortable and would handle any movement from the ship or myself. It was fortunate that my accompanist was Colin Brown. I had met Colin on an earlier trip. He was an excellent classical pianist. That was exactly what was needed to accompany this difficult piece. He was just the capable person to do the accompanying well and as it was meant to be played for the singer. He was simply perfect. It gave me great confidence. Consequently, the aria was sung as well as I have ever sung it, then or now! Fortunately I have a recording of it. This I did play back to my vocal teacher so that she could assess it. Yes, I did get applause, which I loved. Also I must mention that the Master of Ceremonies was a wonderful person by the name of Colin Parker! Thank you, Colin Brown and Colin Parker!

This particular trip found me seated at the doctor's table. This is considered an honor. It was Dr Nigel Roberts. He had been the *Queen Elizabeth*'s chief doctor for many years. In fact, he has written a very interesting book about his days on the *QE2*. His book is titled *C-Six*, a misnomer for the words sea sick! In fact, the dispensary and hospital is located on C stairway, on six deck! The book is appropriately titled. It is interesting reading. I would recommend any *QE2* fan to read the book. To continue, the eminent doctor was an occasional visitor at my table of eight, for dinner. He was a gracious host and we enjoyed his company. Also he was always agreeable to my taking pictures.

While aboard ship we had a truly relaxing time. The sea was its usual calm self. I had never had anything but calm blue sailing on my voyages. Of course, I sail only in the summer months. The passengers aboard were contented and friendly. We had our cocktail party with Captain Bennell. I had grown accustomed to the schedules and procedures. Now, however, we would be arriving in Southampton and making plans to continue on to Norway and Denmark. Even though I had gone to Norway the summer before, this year included Copenhagen, Denmark. There I could see the Tivoli Gardens which I had not seen and was looking forward to seeing.

On the 28th of July, we set sail at 7.30 p.m. for Hellesylt. Then we would let the passengers off who wanted to tour overland and meet us in Geiranger. Of course, being in Geiranger was, for me, the ultimate in rest and relaxation. It would be nice to see the fjords and waterfalls again. We arrived and it was exactly as it had been the year before. The weather was divine and I had the opportunity to buy those things that I had not bought the last time.

We then went on to Trondheim. It is the loveliest, happy Norwegian town. It has shops and restaurants and people actively engaged in their daily activities. I had come wearing my raincoat and carrying the red umbrella from the talent show. It was always a cheerful companion as I traveled alone. The red umbrella and I went into one of the mall-like shopping areas. There in the middle of the mall was a large bronze elephant. It was the type with the large expanded ears. It was such a delight to see there that I had a picture of it with me nearby with the red umbrella.

Our next port of call was Stavanger. The *QE2* docked right at the pier. From the pier we were able to walk to the town. It reminded me of any town at the shore in New Jersey. The shops were up to date in fashion. There was, however, an ethnic difference. Fish markets were in abundance. The locals were busy buying their fish of the day. Also, as one walked along one would often see a statue of a troll or two. The troll seems to be their particular motif for bringing good luck. Of course, I found myself impulsively drawn to the strange-looking trolls and made sure to buy a keyring souvenir with one endearingly hanging from it complete with red hair! At the time that we were there a band came to play for us at the pier. It made us feel special and welcome.

Next we were on to Copenhagen. This would be interesting. Going to the Tivoli Gardens was something to look forward to. Also the tour would take us to see the famous mermaid statue seated on a rock. And, of course, the Moscow Circus!

The heart of Copenhagen is its town square. It is the popular gathering place. Over the doorway of the Town Hall is a statue of Bishop Absalon, the city's founder. The tour was very rewarding. Everything I saw interested me in some way. The square was complete with a band and the changing of the guard. The weather was slightly overcast and the raincoat came in handy, and also my red umbrella, which I shared with a person standing next to me. The rain didn't last long enough to spoil the day. When we entered the Christianborg Castle we saw an impressive throne made entirely of silver!

Then our blue tour bus with the words "Copenhagen Excursions" on it was waiting for us outside. This would take us to the Little Mermaid. One must see it to appreciate it. It was situated in the shallow water off the shore. There on top of a large rock was seated the mermaid! What a pleasure it was to see. One reads about some famous landmark of a country but it is always a surprise to be able to see it.

We were taken for dinner in a French restaurant. It was lovely. Upon entering, you had the impression of being in a rose garden. The tablecloths were a soft green. The chairs at the tables were upholstered in a beautiful rose-patterned chintz. The colors were so appealing that I will long remember having dined there.

After dinner, the main entertainment at the Tivoli Gardens was to see the circus. It was a pleasant evening. The air was warm and sweet. We, the audience, were all standing outside waiting with anticipation for the tour guide to present the tickets. Over the arched entrance door was the word "Circus". Under that was the word "Cirkusbygnunggens". My sister-in-law would have to explain that word since her father came from Denmark. Also there was another sign that read "Moscow Circus". We finally went under the big tent. I loved it. The acrobats swung precariously on the ropes swinging colorful scarves. The musicians were situated on an upper mezzanine of sorts. The entire tent was done to perfection. I laughed and laughed and laughed when the clown came to play the piano and ended up doing the most unimaginable stunts. I really don't know how it's possible to think of that many ways to pull a piano apart and slip and fall! There wasn't a part of the piano that he didn't use to his or our advantage to be funny and he was really funny. Of course, loving the piano as I do, it was a treat just to see it as the focus of attention. We must remember that one of the main reasons I started sailing on the *QE2* was because it had eight pianos aboard!

The next act at the Tivoli Circus was and will remain the most amazing act I have ever seen. To tell you about it, you must visualize the performance ring. It was a ring that was surrounded by a wall about one foot high. At the rear of the performance ring was an entrance or exit curtain. Into the center of the ring came a lady modeling a gorgeous mink coat with a beautiful red fox-fur collar. She modeled the coat by walking around to the romantic music of the band in the mezzanine. It was a lovely sight. However, at the precise moment the cymbal player stood up and clanged his cymbals loudly. At that moment all the mink pieces were suddenly alive and they all scampered across the stage toward the exit curtain. Then to add to our surprise, a fox jumped from around her neck and walked briskly around the wall for all of the audience to see in stunned disbelief. A passenger from the *QE2* who happened to be seated next to me, kept wishing that he had taken his video camera to show the act to his friends back home. I still remember this surprising act and I am glad to tell you about it. I wonder if any of you have seen it. Needless to say, the tour at Copenhagen was wonderful!

Our next port of call was Oslo. It was founded in 1050 by King Harold Haardraade. Oslo is the oldest of the northern capitals. It is also one of the world's largest cities, 175 square miles, though much of it consists of forests and farmland. On the western part of the city is Viegland Park. This park contains sculptures covering every aspect of life. It was created by Gustav Viegland. It has an obelisk in the center of the park which has sculpted humanity forever climbing upward toward the top. It is a very impressive park. We continued on to visit the Town Hall with its monumental painting by Henrik

Sorensen. There were also frescoes, sculptures and wood carvings by other Norwegian artists. The weather in Oslo was so beautiful that I opted to spend time in the sun admiring the flowers. There I remember a couple on their honeymoon from Barcelona, Spain. They enjoyed meeting a person from the United States and I thought it was equally exciting to meet a honeymoon couple from Spain. It causes one to wonder whether the grass is greener on the other side of the fence. Whatever, it was certainly a lovely day in Oslo!

During all of these port city visits life was still buzzing aboard ship. I was now better prepared for the festivities. I had packed not only a pink gown but also a blue gown. Yes, one must be ready for the captain's cocktail party. The captain was Captain Alan Bennell. He invited everyone in the Columbia restaurant to join him and his officers in the Queen's Room. He would then be delighted to meet and be photographed with his guests. Since on the last voyage I wore the pink gown, this time I chose to wear the blue gown. Yes, life was agreeing with me and I was glad to be a part of the festivities. My participation in the cocktail party consisted of drinking orange juice and talking to passengers that I had become acquainted with on the voyage. Many were also table companions for the cruise. Also, I never failed to have my trusty Cameron Sure Shot Camera with me. It was always a good time for taking pictures because everyone was dressed in their formal best. It was also a time to dance, if the desire to do so came about. All in all, we had a good time and went back to our dinner tables ready for a gourmet dinner. Often on formal evenings the ship's photographers would come to each table and take a picture. This would be a nice keepsake as a remembrance.

After the captain's party and our dinner of the evening, it was show time. The Jean Ryan Production Company from Florida would be presenting "Lullaby of Broadway". They were always dressed in appropriate dress for the era. Their songs were great songs from Broadway. Their dancing was superb. I often wondered how they were able to do the intricate dance numbers that required the fellows to lift the girls up on their shoulders. The fact that they were performing on a ship did not seem to bother them one bit. We clapped to encourage them and show our pleasure for their talent. Each song and dance was a treat. Of course, after the show, I made my way to the midnight buffet. There I would have my usual cup of tea. At that time I would find my way to my cabin. If, on the way, I was still interested, I would sit at the piano in the Midships Lobby to play one of my repertoire compositions. I loved doing this!

On some evenings during the Norwegian cruise I enjoyed attending a performance in the theater. If it were a pianist playing classical music, it would be even more pleasing to me. It so happened that one evening at 10 p.m. Colin Brown was scheduled to present a *Norwegian Serenade*. It was billed as a "Special Evening with a Concert Pianist". This concert happened to be held in the Queen's Room. A much more relaxing place for a classical concert. Notwithstanding, the room was filled with an expectant audience, except one elderly gentleman who had fallen asleep during the wait for the concert to begin. I found my seat and waited with great anticipation. I knew Colin as an accompanist for my singing in the talent show and also as a wonderful classical pianist. The grand piano was placed somewhat in the center of the room. It often worried me about how the piano would be steadfast in case of a storm at sea. However, I was told that the legs of the piano were safely encased so as not to allow slipping of any kind.

However, since that time, during rough seas, a grand piano is said to have slid clear across the room. At this time there was no chance of that happening because the sea was calm.

Colin Brown's concert commenced. He played some selections that were on the program for the evening. I do not have that program sheet to tell you exactly the titles of the selections. However, at one point, he said, "I am going to dedicate the next selection to a person I recall wearing a pink evening gown. Her name is Mary Mastony. The name of the composition is *Moonlight Sonata.*" I was certainly surprised that he remembered that I like and played that piece. He had played it before for me in the Yacht Club. Then, after he finished, his next composition was Grieg's *Concerto in A Minor*. This piece, he knew that I had not completed learning the second and third movements. I had showed him my copy of the composition. It was a real inspiration to hear him play it so beautifully all the way through with such great talent. I was totally impressed. Thank you Colin, wherever you may be at this time!

Time was passing by. It would soon be arrival time in Southampton. However, as I stated before, the last day before embarkation was talent show time. Now I would participate again. After all I had studied long and tirelessly for the performance. So it was that I signed up for the show as a participant for the next afternoon. I would be ready first by practicing in my cabin with my tape recorder. Then I would wear the soft flowered dress and carry my tape recorder to tape the performance so that I could play it back later to my singing teacher at Rutgers University. It was exciting to sit and wait for your turn to sing. This time I would have the good fortune to have the marvelous accompanist, Colin Brown. As I typed this, I took time out to hear the tape that I made that day of Friday the 4th of August, 1989. As I listened I was really pleased. The high notes were clear and on the button. Colin accompanied me with such exquisite talent that now I look back and say to my own performance, "Well done." If you the reader happened to be in the audience, I hope you liked it also. You are special to me and I was singing it for your pleasure!

The next day, the 5th of August, 1989, the *Queen Elizabeth II* came into the port of Southampton. Now, we would again have the opportunity to take a bus tour, and of course, see the pier lady. Yes, Elizabeth Taylor was there. We never fail to spot each other. If she is busy at a desk, I go over and greet her. After all, I still remember my first trip to France when she accompanied us, the travelers, to Portsmouth. Now our tour bus would take us to the New Forest, Salisbury, and Stonehenge. The weather was great and just to sit in the bus solo and look out at the English countryside was very appealing for me. Perhaps it reminded me of my first-grade reader that had such lovely cottages in the pictures. My mother did like to read such stories to me when I was even younger. Whatever, I enjoyed the ride. Seeing the spire of the cathedral would forever please me. Also seeing Stonehenge on every trip always caused me to marvel at the construction and ability of the Druids. The entire history came to mind each time, as if it were the first time. After our visit the bus headed back to the ship.

There it was waiting for us in all its glory. We could not help but feel proud that the *QE2* was our destination!

The captain for the return transatlantic crossing was Captain Robin Woodall. This would be the 710th voyage across the Atlantic. To welcome the passengers aboard were Peter Longley, as cruise director, Lindsay Frost, as deputy cruise director, Colin Brown as social director and Elaine Mackay, as part of the cruise staff. With such a fine crew in charge, we would be assured of a good trip.

I had a room change for the return. The first thing I did was to relocate and then get my belongings in place. Then on with the trip. In the Grand Lounge there was a special presentation featuring the Michelmersh Silver Band. Then later, at 2.30 p.m. the gangways were raised. The Michelmersh Silver Band was on the pier to play us away. After that there was a commentary on the open deck as the *Queen Elizabeth II* sailed down the Solent. I was there to take pictures. It was always sad to leave England and Southampton. It would take another year before I would have the chance to see the port again!

The host of my table was again the ship's doctor. However, the first night he would not be with us. We had a congenial group. After dinner and with a luscious piece of chocolate in my mouth, I went to the Grand Lounge to watch show time. This evening a magician and an illusionist were being featured. Magic shows are a great form of entertainment. It is a sure way to forget all of the necessities we have in life. I liked seeing the doves appear from what looked like nowhere! Each magician has a special presentation. I remember one act I saw on the *QE2*. It was an illusion. The magician held up a polka-dot scarf. He shook the scarf and all of the polka dots fell off! He shook the scarf again and the dots returned. Great! It didn't take much to amuse me on vacation! After the show there was the usual midnight buffet. Then with a few songs at the piano and adjusting my watch one hour back, I was off to dreamland! I always sleep well at sea!

Next day was a Sunday. After the boat drill that was held for the new passengers, I hurried to the theater. On Sunday, Captain Robin Woodall would conduct the Interdenominational Divine Service. His presentation and the Hymn to Sailors was beautiful and reassuring. I would not miss a Captain Woodall church service, then or on my following trips. Thank you, Captain Woodall!

At the noon hour, complimentary dance classes were held. In general I never attended the classes. I do like to dance and have participated in all forms of dancing as an adult. There was modern dance, ballet, tap, and of course social dancing. The teachers were the McCormicks, Debbie and Steve. I thought they were exceptional dancers. Also their costumes were really outstanding. Later, I was told by Debbie, that her mother made all of her lovely gowns. She also said that her mother made the beautifully tailored suits that her husband wore. Debbie was such a nice person, as was Steve. However, Debbie was special because she often had her hair arranged so that a curl was right in the middle of her forehead. When I commented about how pretty it was, she told me that the curl was glued to her forehead for dance performances. I liked that bit of trivia. Whatever, I joined the dance class and had some dances with the professional Steve McCormick. Great dancing. Thank you, Steve and Debbie!

It was my custom to circle any activity for the day that interested me. So it was that at 3.15 p.m. in the Grand Lounge there was an informal talk *"QE2 and Cunard"*. This was to be about the *QE2* and the Cunard Shipping Line. The talk was held by cruise director, Peter Longley. Quite a number of passengers gathered to hear the presentation. It was most interesting. Peter Longley had great command of the English language and a fascinating way of telling the story of the ship and the Cunard Line. I liked his lectures and attended others that followed on my voyages. Thank you, Peter!

For some unknown reason, I never attended the scheduled group meetings of Single or Traveling Alone, of which I was both. I enjoyed meeting all of the many interesting people aboard. Unexpected meetings seemed so much more interesting. Also I got so completely involved in one, two, or three of the arts, that there was never enough time. To each his own, they say.

There were different activities on the hour and the half hour and in between. There was enough variety to satisfy any traveler. Then when you finally returned to your cabin to prepare for dinner, the television in the cabin always had an interesting program to be aware of as you dressed.

This particular evening we had the special invitation from Captain Robin Woodall cordially inviting those of us who dined in the Queens Grill, Princess Grill, and the Columbia restaurant to join him and his officers for cocktails in the Queen's Room from 6.45 p.m. to 7.45 p.m. The captain would receive his guests at the forward portside entrance to the library. That same evening there was a dance in the Columbia restaurant. I dressed in a long sky-blue gown that I had worn to Captain Bennell's party. As I was on my way, I came to the staircase and waited there for a party of four people who were coming up the steps, four abreast. As I stood at the top waiting in my blue gown, one of the ladies looked up and said, "It's the Virgin Mary!" It was Sunday and perhaps she was still thinking of church. I don't think that she knew that my name really was Mary! For whatever reason, I have kept the incident in my mental computer to reflect upon!

The captain's party is always resplendent with beautifully dressed people and happy faces. The hors d'oeuvres table is a happy meeting place. We listen to the music, talk to friends and enjoy the introduction of the captain's officers. One never tires of the captain's parties. Sometimes, you are even lucky enough to receive a small gold trimmed invitation to a party held for passengers who have traveled on the *QE2* on former trips. These parties are held in the captain's quarters or the officer's quarters on the upper deck. On one occasion I received two invitations to both parties that were being held on the same night at the same time. I found myself being joyfully pulled from one party to the other. It was a cheerful situation!

Some days aboard ship were called nautical days. These were the days that we were at sea with no port of call. We were now on passage to New York. It was nautical day. There were many interesting lectures and activities planned. What I liked best was the informal interview by Elaine Mackay with Captain Robin Woodall, Master of the *QE2*.

He was such a capable captain that I felt safe aboard the ship when he was at the helm. Thank you, Elaine and Captain Woodall!

At 10.15 there was a special evening with pianist Colin Brown. I did list the program of his pieces on my daily schedule. It was as follows: *Fantasy in D Minor* by Mozart, *Impromptu* by Schubert, *Arabesque in A Major* by Debussy, *Moonlight Sonata* by Beethoven and *Nocturne in B Flat Minor* by Chopin. It was glorious music. I am so proud to write that the following day he was my accompanist in the talent show. Applause for Colin Brown!

The next evening there was another concert pianist playing in the theater. His name was Eric Mechanic. I went to hear him perform. There was Colin Brown at the entry door. When he saw me, he asked what I would be singing in the talent show. I said I didn't know. He suggested that I sing Puccini's *O Mio Babbino Caro*. To which I replied that I wasn't sure that the audience would like it because the girl wanted to commit suicide by jumping off a bridge. To which Colin replied that I could try singing it from the mezzanine balcony of the ship! We both laughed. Very funny!

It was now the last day before disembarkation for New York City. The time had come for me to prepare for the talent show. One fact was sure, Colin Brown would accompany me. This made everything much easier for me because I am always apprehensive about having the right accompaniment. Some of the popular pianists have not had any expertise in classical opera.

The talent show would also have a very professional master of ceremony. He was Colin Parker. He knew exactly how to present a person who was about to perform. With all of this confidence, and wearing my flowered dress and ballet slippers, I was indeed ready. As I documented this for you, the reader, I went to my trusty recorder to hear exactly how I was presented, how my accompanist supported and embellished the music and how I hit the high notes. It was perfect! I would say it was the best along with the other two shows of this particular cruise! Never would I, in my estimation, sound as good as that year of 1989.

The aria that I sang was *O Mio Babbino Caro*, translated it is "O My Dear Daddy". This aria is about a young girl who must ask her father for permission to marry. She tells her father how much she is in love. She is so much in love that she wants to go to the Port of Roses to buy a wedding ring. Then she goes on to tell her father that if he doesn't give her permission, she will go to the Old Bridge and throw herself into the Arno River. She is so tormented that she wishes that she could die. "Father," she says, "please have pity, pity, pity!" The aria is truly beautiful and it is the first aria that I fell in love with.

To continue with the talent show, it was introduced by Colin Parker. I came forward and told the audience that I would sing *O Mio Babbino Caro* and also *Quando Me'n Vo*. Both arias were composed by Puccini. I sang and Colin accompanied me beautifully. I dedicated the *O Mio Babbino Caro* to Colin Brown. He had requested it. Then I sang *Quando Me'n Vo*. This is a happy aria about a young girl who goes out walking and feeling very sure of her beauty and the glances she

A teacher friend Larry escorting me to the QE2 pier in New York – 1986.

Musical moment with Colin Brown.

Singing *Nel Cor Pui Non Si Sento*. Note the bag from Portugal.

In the receiving line to meet Captain Bennell – 1987.

Ready with music for the accompanist to sing the beautiful *O Mio Babbino Caro*.

Time to relax in spectacular Geirenger Fjord – 1988.

Singing *Quando Me'n Vo Soletta* (When I Go Alone).

Stonehenge and New Forest tour.

receives. It is Muzette's waltz from the opera *La Boheme*. At the end of each aria I received the applause I liked. After all, the *QE2* passengers were the perfect audience! Thank you, one and all!

On went the transatlantic sailing into my home port. Another wonderful summer came to a close!

Chapter Six
Cunard Line's 150th Anniversary 1990

Hip, hip, hooray! What a wonderful expectation! This would be the celebration year of the 150th Anniversary of the Cunard Line! Splendid programs were being planned including a visit aboard ship by Her Royal Highness!

To proceed with the events leading up to this great vacation, I must mention a few of the preparations. Most of it was spent in the music department of Rutgers University. I was now deeply committed to voice study. My teacher was working toward a doctorate in musicology besides teaching voice classes. I attended the voice classes and also took private lessons for one hour each week. She was extremely well-qualified and an expert teacher of voice. I continued to take lessons after she received her degree and became a professor of voice at a New York College of the Arts. Also, I was taking the opera workshop class with the director of the opera department. I was simply enchanted with opera. The beautiful soprano arias were both beautiful in composition and in the sweet and expressive way of telling about situations in life. Thank you Dr Jacklyn Schneider, my great teacher, and Dr Valerie Goodall, director of the opera department at Rutgers!

At Rutgers any phase of piano composition was on my schedule. The harmony classes went far beyond what I had learned. Every class was a challenge. Jazz was not overlooked. I liked improvisations on the piano and had the opportunity to attend class with a great jazz performer from New York. However, my preference was for the classics, and that, to this day, is what I enjoy most.

Besides voice and piano, I had classes in modern dance. This form of dance I was particularly fond of because I participated in it during my undergraduate days at Penn State University. My dance teacher was a professional dancer and teacher from New York. The creative dance classes under her auspices I shall never forget. On one occasion we were required to make a presentation before the students. I composed a dance that embodied voice, piano and dance. The voice lesson I had been working on had been from Verdi's *Un Ballo in Maschera,* "The Masked Ball". I presented it in dance form representative of the page boy protective of the king. Then, in the middle of the presentation, I quickly changed into a black cat by using my long black sash as a tail. I had my trusty tape recorder already placed on the floor and at the proper moment turned it on to play some common scales. Then in time to each note I pretended that I was a cat walking on the keys of a piano. The class and the teacher liked it. Thank you, Professor Gittleman!

So my year rolled on until summer and *QE2* time! This voyage would be special since the Queen of England would be aboard. It was a gorgeous day on 17th July, 1990. A white stretch limousine came to take me to the pier in New York. Larry, my teacher friend, came with me to bid me a happy voyage. I was going in style. After all I was going to board my favorite ship and I was going to see the Queen. I wore a white lace-trimmed dress and a pretty white lace-brimmed sun-hat that I carried. Life was worth living!

Once on deck, festivities began that did not ordinarily take place on other trips. However, this was a Royal trip, was it not?

There was a blue band playing stirring band music. There were blue and white balloons tied to the light posts. From the deck we had been given red, white and blue streamers to throw. There was a sailaway party on the Lido deck. There the "150 Greatest Hits" were being played to celebrate the beginning of the Cunard Line's 150 years anniversary!

First things first, that is boat drill! After arriving in your cabin, you immediately look for your life saving jacket. A great vest-like orange-colored jacket is what you must wear. Then you proceed to walk up the stairs where your deck level group will meet. There you are informed as to the procedure you follow in case of any emergency at sea. When I arrived at my station I found the eminent journalist Edwin Newman there also. We checked to see that our jackets were tied properly and he allowed me to take a picture of him in the life-jacket. One of my first ambitions was to become a journalist. However, I opted for teaching because there were more jobs available. However, I never lost my interest in journalism or story-telling. It is a pleasure for me to write and type, which is exactly what I am doing at this very minute!

On this crossing we were fortunate to have the orchestra of the Academy of St Martin in the Fields. It is a great orchestra and I was pleased to attend the performance at 9.15 p.m. in the Grand Lounge. The musicians played so well that the audience appreciated every selection with great applause. After the concert, in the Queen's Room was held the Transatlantic Colors Ball. I was ready for this because it had been advertised in my brochure before starting the trip. I had a rose-colored gown with white off-the-shoulder flounce trim. It was a dress perfect for the occasion. The steward of my room said I looked divine!

That put me in a good mood. At my table, for this crossing, sat a fellow passenger who was also a travel agent for the trip. He was attired beautifully in his tuxedo. So it happened that I had a dance partner for the evening. He was not only a dance partner, but also the fastest and liveliest partner I have ever had in my life. We really cut a rug!

The next day in the theater "Comedy", an informal lecture by Tony Randall, was presented by host Edwin Newman. Tony Randall was a popular award winning actor of stage, screen and television. The auditorium was filled to the rafters. It was great for the passengers to see in person stars they had only known or seen in the movies. It made for an interesting afternoon.

This was the special evening for people seated in the Columbia restaurant. We were invited to Captain Robin Woodall's cocktail party. It was always a highlight of the voyage to meet the Captain and his officers. Captain Woodall had a nice calming approach. We liked that. I did, because I was always just that wee bit apprehensive about being at sea, even though I had made perfect trips. I took pictures, chatted and enjoyed the evening!

For entertainment that evening the Cunard Line presented the comedy of the Smothers Brothers. I had heard them on my television set at home. Now it would be great to see them in person. They were their usual funny selves. Each brother complimenting the other in comic dialogue and situations. They were also good musicians, one on the bass and one on the guitar. At the midnight buffet, I was surprised to see then there. They offered to have me join them at their table. I reluctantly did so and was glad that I had actually talked to these comic stars. Of course, I got a picture also. It is a nice memory. I appreciate it. Thank you, Smothers Brothers!

The *QE2* had its own masked ball. It was a colorful affair with music by the Peter Duchin Orchestra. I wore an ankle length pink gown and mask of gold-colored sequins. Others were dressed in costumes representing some character or personality. It was a fun affair. Prizes were awarded to the most interesting masquerader. After the ball when I went to bed I found a blue card on my pillow. It was a reminder to adjust our watches before retiring. Sailing east-bound we advanced our clocks one hour each night. There is a five hour difference between New York and England.

The last day before reaching Southampton had arrived! Also it was the day of the talent show. One is constantly busy aboard. It was time for me to report for the rehearsal at 11 a.m. Since Colin Brown was not on board, I had to go over my aria with a piano player I did not know. It went well. The selection was the beautiful *Caro Nome*, by Verdi.

At 4 p.m. the talent show would begin. I had the routine well in mind. First I would practice with the tape recorder to warm up. Then I would select a dress to wear. I enjoyed making that decision. Clothes have always been a form of art for me. The dress decided upon was a black and white one. The top was a flouncy white organdy with drop shoulders, The skirt was a full black net-like material with a crinoline underskirt. It was quite nice but not what I usually like to wear. I seem to tend toward the pastels or florals. Whatever, I sang and recorded the singing with my little recorder on stage with me. It went well. I sang *Caro Nome*. The applause was great and I was pleased. When I had finally gone to my room to hear what it sounded like, I was doubly pleased. It was perfect according to what I had learned. I was pleased with the singing and the applause.

Onward! At this point, in my writing, I would like to tell you that I have the daily programs for the past ten years of trips. I have diaries since 1988. I have ten large photograph albums depicting every phase of the yearly trips. Thus, at this time I have all the reference material that I need. Besides all of this, I have a built in typist; that is me! The typewriter presently being used is an electric typewriter, new and pleasant to type on. Of course, I could use a computer. I'll look at some. However, typing on the one I now have is so pleasant and it feels a bit like playing the piano!

We reached Southampton and there was no time for a tour. Since my camera was out of film, I decided to go ashore and buy some film and also call my brother and family to let them know that I had arrived. To my delight, guess who I met up with? Yes, the pier lady Elizabeth Taylor. At this point she offered her address and I gave her my calling card. We never did have occasion to correspond. After all, the fun was in the yearly surprise meeting! Then, after that meeting I called my brother's home. Telling him about how great the trip had been was always satisfying to me and my brother's family. By the way, it was ninety degrees in England that day!

Such excitement! We were now embarking on our main cruise around the British Isles. The Light Infantry Salamanca Band played a special embarkation concert. We were all in a festive mood. The gangways were raised at 4 p.m. and shortly afterwards the *Queen Elizabeth II* set sail for Cobh, Ireland, a distance of 314 nautical miles. Then at 6 p.m. some passengers joined in the Grand Lounge to sing "Songs of Praise". These were well-known hymns that were being filmed to be broadcast later on the BBC. Then later in the evening an Irish comedy star was featured on show time. It put passengers in an Irish frame of mind. I had relatives living in Ireland who would receive a card from me when we arrived in Cobh.

It was a beautiful day and warm and pleasant when we arrived in Cobh. Just to watch the tugs pulling us into port was a thrill. We landed. I started on my tour. We went to Cork to see Blarney Castle. I had been there before, so it was a double pleasure to see it again. However, just seeing the throngs of people who had come to see the *QE2* in dock was unbelievable. I managed to send a card to my in-laws, but somehow I thought they were in the crowd looking for me. Later the ship would have a picture of some of the ports visited and perhaps I would see them in it! The city of Cobh that we had visited is pronounced "Cove". It is situated on the southern shore of Ireland and is one of the world's finest harbors. From the port of Cobh, many emigrants left Ireland to seek their fortunes in the New World.

On board we had a demonstration of traditional Irish folk dancing. We were all aboard and ready for the evening's activities before going on to our next port of call. This evening Captain Woodall invited the passengers in the Columbia restaurant to join him and his officers for cocktails. It was a wonderful way to end a perfect day. In my suitcase I had brought a beautiful gown for the occasion. It was a white brocade satin gown, floor length, in three levels. The top was held by one wide shoulder piece that extended to the middle of the back. I simply felt very good and festive for the evening. Of course, I accepted all the photographs that the *QE2* photographers took that evening. Finally, after five trips, I was dressed in a manner comparable to the beautiful *QE2* ship! Later on that evening was held another grand masked ball. I simply carried the hand-held sequined mask.

We arrived at Liverpool on Tuesday, 24th July, 1990. The *QE2* anchored at approximately 11.30 a.m. off Pier Head. There were 10,000 red and blue balloons released off the one deck to celebrate this inaugural visit of the *QE2* to Liverpool. I reserved a tour at 1.30 p.m. called "City of Surprises". It was, according to my diary, a beautiful, beautiful day! Our tour bus drove us all around Liverpool. This was the home of those famous Beatles. Well, it was quite a city! The churches were a highlight. They were truly lovely. We were shown the church that the Beatles had attended. In the large park-like area at the edge of the town all the local people seemed to have turned out to welcome the *Queen Elizabeth II*. After all, this was Cunard's first home port. In the center of town was a large building called the Cunard Building. Also, I had learned that Liverpool was the home town of Captain Robin Woodall. I don't know if I am correct about this. It was a great city and I liked having the opportunity to see it.

That night, in the port of Liverpool, at 10.45 p.m. was a celebration of fireworks. The display was fabulous. In my daily account, I had written, "Wow, what a show!" It was a lovely summer evening in which to enjoy the spectacle. I would be looking forward to the video that was being prepared for the passengers to order as a remembrance of this voyage!

It had been a great day which also included a "Celebration 150 – Cunard's Celebrated 150 Years of Sailing". This was a show presented in the Grand Lounge. It was a sparkling showtime review with the Jean Ann Ryan Singers and Dancers. What a wonderful voyage thus far!

Next stop, Greenock. It was the birthplace of the *QE2*. It was built on the ways of John Brown's shipyard. It was there that it plunged for the first time into the Clyde. After being named by Her Majesty the Queen, the new liner *Queen Elizabeth II* entered the River Clyde on 20th September, 1967. It must have been a privilege to have had an admission ticket to John Brown's Shipyard for the launch of *TSS Queen Elizabeth II* on that day!

At 9 a.m. the *QE2* docked at the container terminal at Greenock. Out on the open decks we could hear the pipe and drum band on the quayside and watched the mounted police branch display. Of course, I never forgot my first enchantment with Scotland, and I was looking forward to being there.

My tour was called "Ayr and Burns Country". I chose this tour because when I was a child my mother read his poetry to me. I shall never forget her reading of *Coming Through the Rye*. I well remember the book that she read. It was about six by six inches in size. It was padded and had an oval opening with a flowered insert. The pages were glossy white, with an occasional etching. The one I liked had a little girl walking happily through the rye. I loved the book, I loved the picture and I loved my mother. As a tribute to her, I present the poem:

COMING THROUGH THE RYE

Coming through the rye, poor body,
Coming through the rye,
She draiglet a, her petticoatie.
Coming through the rye.

Gin a body meet a body
Coming through the rye;
Gin a body kiss a body,
Need a body cry.

Gin a body meet a body
Coming through the glen
Gina body kiss a body,
Need the worl ken?

Jenny's a, wat, poor body;
Jenny's seldom dry;
She draiglet a, her petticoatie,
Coming through the rye.

On my mother's knee, I loved the poem about the little girl, the kiss, the cry and the petticoatie! She knew I liked it. I knew she also loved reading it to me. My mother was so very good to me!

Now I was having the opportunity to see Robert Burns' cottage. Believe me, I looked forward to it with great anticipation. It met my expectations. I even kept the ticket to the entrance of his home in my photo book!

We were then taken to a Scottish hotel near a golf course. Here we had lunch and were given a small sample bottle of Scotch. it would make a nice gift on my return home. After dinner, a large chorus gathered on the green to sing farewell songs to us. Is it any wonder that I get misty-eyed when I think of Scotland and the privileges I have received by traveling on the *QE2*?

At 3.30 p.m. it was "All Aboard" time. The gangways were raised and shortly afterwards, the *Queen Elizabeth II* set sail for Cherbourg, France. In the meantime, there were special performances by entertainers aboard. Then in the evening, at 10.15 p.m. in the theater there was a recital featuring Christina Ortiz. She was a pianist from South America. Listening to her classical repertoire was a good way to end a great day! Of course, the midnight buffet was not missed! As I enjoyed the usual midnight fare, strains of Franz Liszt's *Liebestraum* were replaying in my brain, because I also played that composition in my recital back home.

We are now on our way again on this "armchair saga". The next port of call was Cherbourg. Now everyone aboard is beginning to know that it won't be long before the Queen will be coming aboard.

We would dock at Cherbourg at 2 p.m. at the Gare Maritime. The weather continued to be beautiful. In the morning I heard an informal lecture in the theater titled

"Cunard's 150 Glorious Years – The Middle Years". John Maxtome-Graham, noted maritime historian, gave the lecture. I found it very interesting and appropriate for this trip!

We arrived at Cherbourg. As I walked toward the shopping area near the pier, a Frenchman approached me. He was holding a microphone.

He said, "You have just come off the ship, no? Did you have a special celebration?"

I was startled to hear him speak to me and with a microphone in his hand. I was also surprised because I detected a number of French words that I didn't comprehend. Should I answer in French or English?

Finally I answered, "Oui, oui, c'est trés magnifique!"

After all this was my chance to use Madame Forbinger's French lesson. Well, the man responded totally in French! Now, I was at something of a loss. However, I replied with a mixture of English and French similar to that he had inflicted on me at the beginning. So we continued for a while, as I watched other *QE2* passengers pass by, looking at this impromptu interview. Finally I departed. Some passengers met up with me. They said, "I see you were on French television!" Well, well, is that what was going on? Apparently the French were joining in on the Cunard celebration by joyfully interviewing the passengers. I happened to be the unsuspecting one!

The tour that I selected was to Barfleur. It sounded like a nice place full of flowers. After all, I did know that fleur meant flower. I wasn't sure about the "bar" part of the city's name. It turned out to be representative of both parts of the word!

The bus tours very often take the tourists to some remote towns. I do believe it is to take care of the parking problem. Whatever, we were taken up the mountain to La Pennel. This was a place where we had a good view of the whole of France! I'm exaggerating, of course. However, I did find myself looking at the beautiful panorama. The one church that was there was small and better-looking from the outside! The chief calling card for being there was that we would be served French crêpes for afternoon tea. We all lined up for this delicacy. It was a considerable line which must have seemed even longer to the French lady who was cooking the crêpes, individually, as we approached her. I could tell that she was getting exasperated. Here, in this rural region in the mountain, I don't believe she was used to having her haute cuisine rushed! Whatever, she began raising her strong, heavy voice to her helpers in the kitchen, to get on with more and more provisions. I received my crêpe and went outdoors to eat it alone, in the sunshine!

We went back to the little fishing village, Barfleur, where the bus stopped to allow us to walk around a bit and look at the fishing boats. This place was not Paris. By this time I needed a restroom. What to do? What to do? "Mary," I said to myself, "look in the restaurants. There you will surely find a place." This I did, but to my surprise they were mainly bars that I would not feel free to enter. If I did, I wouldn't really know how to ask for a restroom. What to do? What to do? I walked on. Finally I saw a string of what we Americans call "outhouses". We all know about these little houses. What we don't always know or like to know, is that they consist mainly of a hole in the floor in France. However, the time had come. It was now or never! I braced myself to go into one. Well, there were so many flies to greet my arrival, I had to flee in panic. A passerby noticed my situation and wisely came to my rescue. She directed me to her bus, she showed me that they had a small restroom on board. I was profoundly grateful. I quickly went into the cubicle. As I left, I thanked her for her kindness!

When we returned to the shopping center near the pier, I went shopping for bottles of perfume. This had nothing to do with the last experience! Now, at the pier, I saw a performance of accordion music and dancing, going on. It set a French atmosphere for us. I bought some brand name perfumes, like Chanel. Also, I bought lovely boxes of French milled soaps. Now back on the *QE2*. Thank heaven!

It was destined to be a great night of anticipation. There was a feeling of togetherness. The evening's entertainment was to be held in the Grand Lounge. Scheduled was the Royal Philharmonic Orchestra, conducted by André Previn. I had heard him conduct on television. This was an opportunity to see and hear him perform. His program was totally Beethoven, one of my favorite composers. Had he not composed the *Moonlight Sonata*? The numbers on the program were: *Overture Coriolan*, *Symphony #4*, *Adagio-Allegro*, *Allegro Vivace*, and *Allegro Ma Non Troppo*. It was a great program and I certainly enjoyed the evening of listening.

After a fine day and an evening of music, we all went on deck at 11 p.m. to observe the fireworks. A great display of color sparkled in the night sky. There is nothing more exciting for a festivity than fireworks. After all, the Queen would be on board tomorrow. We had all been given a card from the Cunard Line. It gave the protocol in the presence of Her Majesty and His Highness, The Duke of Edinburgh. Protocol stated that we were not to approach the Royal couple, but wait to be approached. If we did meet we would please bow and curtsey. We would shake hands only if offered. If we were speaking to Her Majesty, she was to be addressed as "Your Majesty." In subsequent conversation Her Majesty is addressed as "Ma'am". His Royal Highness the Duke of Edinburgh would be addressed as "Sir".

The special day arrived. It was a bit misty but nice. We practiced our HOORAYS with a staff member. There would be three Hip, Hip, Hips, then we would follow with a loud HOORAY. This was to be done three times when we saw Her Majesty and the Duke of Edinburgh!

A Royal review of the Cunard Fleet would be made by Her Majesty the Queen. The *QE2* anchored at 8.15 a.m. Then a steam past of Cunard and Royal Naval vessels sailed in the Solent. They would then be reviewed by the Queen from Her Majesty's yacht Britannia. Approximately every fifteen minutes ships came in to anchor. First some larger ships. Then the small ships came in to anchor. At about 9.25 a.m. the Royal Squadron sailed from Portsmouth. First was the Trinity House vessel Oatrucua, followed by Her Majesty's yacht Britannia, followed by Her Majesty's army vessel Broadsword.

At 10.45 a.m., we were ready for the invitation to participate in giving "Three cheers for Her Majesty The Queen". At the precise moment the command over the public address system was heard. "Stand by to give three cheers". Upon hearing the words "Three cheers for her Majesty The Queen – hip, hip, hip" we all joined in on the HOORAY! This was repeated three times. It was very exciting. I took as many pictures as I could get to put in my album when I returned home.

The best of the Queen's visit was yet to come. Concorde, Britannia Airways 767, and Heavy Lift Belfast, Virgin Airways 747 flew past. Then the Royal yacht Britannia anchored and Her Majesty the Queen and His Royal Highness prepared to disembark on to the *QE2*. At noon, the Royal party embarked for luncheon on board the *QE2*.

On all of the deck levels that Her Majesty and His Royal Highness walked, we were allowed to stand and watch as they passed by. I tried to get a good viewing area. It was not easy because we had no knowledge of where they might be walking on their way to lunch. I finally found a viewing spot right by the Grand Lounge stage. Her Majesty was approaching. I was enthralled. She came closer and closer. When she came within one foot of where I was standing, she gave me the most beautiful smile! I will never forget it! I could not believe I had seen the Queen and that she had smiled at me. I will always remember the moment. Even as a child I remember reading in my books about visiting the Queen and how wonderful it was. Now I had seen the Queen and she smiled a beautiful smile! The 150th Anniversary voyage was worth it beyond my imagination. Thank you, Your Royal Highness, for the lovely smile!

At 4.15 p.m. the Royal Party disembarked from the *QE2*. Then all of us aboard continued with the scheduled celebrations. After our dinner we had entertainment in the Grand Lounge of music and dance. Then in the theater was a concert of light classics. The Royal Philharmonic Orchestra was performing. At 10.45 p.m. a Royal ball was held in the Queen's Room that was elaborately decorated for the event. Finally there was a fireworks display on the open decks. It was another wonderful day aboard the *QE2*!

On Saturday the 28th of July the *QE2* set sail for New York. The day was beautiful. I decided to put on my bathing suit and simply wiggle my toes in the hot tub on deck. I am a good swimmer. I have been swimming since I was a child of six, when I wore a home-made bathing suit. Later in college I was part of the lifeguard class. Now, I don't want to get wet. Water destroys my hair. I just like the sunshine!

The evening was much the same as usual. The Grand Lounge featured the Jean Ryan Dancers and Singers in a presentation of the Follies Parisienne. It was a colorful presentation and happy music. The audience always seem to like the cancan dance. They performed it in jolly good fun. Then after the show was over, I changed "classes", as I like to call it, and I went to the next "class", the midnight buffet for the usual snack. Again it was another great day at sea!

For the return sailing, Captain Robin Woodall would be conducting the Interdenominational Divine Service. As I mentioned before, I never missed his service if I was lucky enough to be aboard on a Sunday. As Master of the *QE2*, he always presented the service with great dignity. I would wait for the time to sing the Hymn to the Sailors. It seemed to give me a chance to mentally thank the navigators, of all times, including those of the *QE2*. Thank you sailors for all of my safe trips on the *QE2*.

On Sunday afternoon white caps could be seen on the ocean, and the sea seemed a bit rough but nothing disturbing. The day was spent enjoying friends, entertainment, practicing the piano, whenever it was quiet in the Midships Lobby, and in general enjoying being aboard.

In the evening, in the Queen's Room, the Bootlegger's ball was held. The name fascinated me. It was an informal dance that was supposed to represent a bygone era. I simply wore a black skirt with a short sleeved black and white cotton top. I felt comfortable. A passenger had a foot-long cigarette holder to emphasize the look of the time. She allowed me to take a picture of myself holding it. Then, I felt part of the Bootlegger's ball.

Don't forget to adjust your clocks and watches before retiring at night! Yes, we were again changing our time at night so that we would be in sync with New York time when we arrived there. I always made sure to do so and also to call the Purser's Office to give me a wake up call at 6. a.m. I am an early riser even when I turn in late, which I certainly did every night on the *QE2*. There were so many wonderful activities!

Here are some of the activity programs that were available, some of which I participated in and some I didn't. I always had an aerobic suit with me and I attended the classes on six deck, F stairway. I liked the classes but seemed to prefer jogging or walking on open deck in the mornings. I would get a pre-breakfast orange juice and proceed to enjoy the sea air. If no one was nearby, I would sing an aria of my choice. An aria sung to the sea is very rewarding. Somehow it seems as though that is exactly where humans were meant to sing of the joy of life!

What I did not participate in was playing bridge or lectures about bridge, I had never learned the game or wished to do so. However, this does not discredit those who enjoy the game. However, if it is played for money, my parents would have totally disapproved. Which takes me to another activity aboard – gambling. The casinos aboard are lovely, with decor and sophisticated ladies. Those who enjoy the machines or tables seem to be possessed by "playing". I never could quite understand that gambling with money was a form of playing. I worked too hard teaching to ever think of gambling with my earnings. Also, I never took part in the horseracing, which was another form of gambling. So it went for the no-nos, for me!

The day would be festive because Captain Woodall was inviting the passengers in the Queen's Grill, Princess Grill and the Columbia restaurant to join him and his senior officers for cocktails in the Queen's Room from 7 p.m. to 8 p.m. I continued to enjoy this special affair. For this trip I was seated at a table with a couple from Massachusetts. Since I was born in Massachusetts, we had interesting table conversation. The evening went by pleasantly. Since it was captain's night pictures were taken at the dining tables. I was wearing the black and white ankle length dress.

For the evening's entertainment we had Rich Little. He is an impressionist and comedian. I have heard him on television. He is quite a funny fellow. This evening he chose to impersonate Groucho Marx by first putting on a mustache and then proceeding to impersonate the notorious comic. However, what I enjoyed most was when he impersonated our then president, Ronald Reagan. At that time the president was having a problem with Nicaragua. It was called the Contra Affair. The president had not been quite sure of the policies he had to deal with. Rich Little made fine funny use of this bit of trivia. "If we had known, what we should have known, but didn't know that we knew we had known before we knew that we knew that we had really not known," etc., etc. Thus, Rich Little went on with his imitation of President Reagan. I found it very funny!

The sea that day had been rather choppy. I spent a little time in the cabin. To my surprise, I received a telephone call from the lady from Australia who I had met on my first trip on the *QE2* in 1985. She knew that I had taken the 150th anniversary trip and decided to call me aboard ship all the way from Australia. I told her that we were having a wonderful time. However, part of the wonderful time was that a friend would call all the way from Australia to greet me while aboard ship. She had since married a Lord and she was now titled Lady Ann. Thank you, Lady Ann!

Time certainly passes quickly! I recall my Dean of Women at Penn state saying to our class, "Girls, the most important thing in life is time." Then again, "Girls the most important thing in life is time." She repeated it to make sure we absorbed her offering of wisdom. So it is that I value my time and have a feeling of surprise to know that time is passing and quickly! Thank you, Dean Charlotte Ray!

Speaking of time, it was time once again for the talent show. The rehearsal was held in the morning and the show was at 4 p.m. Since I had been vocalizing all year in classes and private lessons, I knew exactly what I would sing and I made sure to have the music for anyone who might accompany me. At this time I don't recall who the accompanist was. I do know the arias that I sang. One was a favorite *O Mio Babbino Caro* and the other was a new arietta called *Il Bacio (The Kiss)*. How many hours I practiced that sweet song, knowing that it surely was meant to be sung for the *QE2* passengers. The song tells of a girl who says that nothing in the world is more important than a kiss. She would gladly give up all her expensive jewelry, because that is of no importance. She thought the important treasure was the kiss. For this song I wore a rose-flowered chintz dress. I also wore a long opera-length string of pearls. With myself in readiness, and my recorder in hand, I waited my turn on the program. When my turn came, I sang with the feeling I have for the aria. When I sang *Il Bacio*, and came to the part where the jewelry was of no importance to me, I pretended to throw off my long string of pearls. I think the audience was pleased. I was pleased. I have the recording of it to remember the moment. The pianist was very good. I am so pleased when it works so well at such short notice with the accompanist. Thank you!

Now everything was downhill. It was time to make plans for getting off the ship the next morning. There were some technicalities, however, besides packing. It was gratuity time, so off to the purser's deck, on deck two. With the gratuities in envelopes I could concentrate on simply enjoying the last day of this wonderful voyage.

There were various activities scheduled, one would be hard-pressed to attend them all. However, Captain Woodall said we were approaching a storm called Hurricane Bertha. I knew Bertha meant big. There is a large piece of machinery that is named "Big Bertha". Whatever, I was apprehensive, first the Captain said we would alter the course, which would add five hours to our arrival time. Then it was necessary to add another two hours. It was good to know that we had a great captain who knew exactly what to do in such disturbing weather conditions. I felt confident with Captain Woodall at the helm. Thank you, Captain Woodall for our safe voyage!

At dinner, on the last night, we have a special affair given by the waiters. It is called Baked Alaska Night. That is the evening when we have a special celebration with sparklers on top of baked Alaska cakes. Amid the fanfare of rousing music, the waiters hold the sparkling cakes above their heads as they march in line. Around the dining room flags of every nation are displayed to add to the festivities. When we finally have the marvelous ice cream desert, that is baked in its whipped egg-white covering, one more ingredient is added. The extra ingredient was a sauce of gorgeous warmed red cherries! It is the perfect compliment to send off all of the passengers. The waiters have certainly earned their gratuities. Thank you, and three cheers! If you have never traveled on the *QE2*, I hope you are sold on it now.

It had been a great day regardless of the weather. Also, we had a presentation in the Grand Lounge of the Royal Philharmonic Orchestra led by André Previn. It was unique in that toy instruments were played by the cruise staff at various intervals during a selection. It was musical and entertaining as well. Thank you, cruise staff!

Last, but not least, we had a gala farewell ball. It was an informal affair in which we could talk to friends and reminisce about the great trip that it had been. The hors d'oeuvres were abundant, and the decor was lavish with stellar motifs. The music by the Bobby Rosengarden Orchestra was superb. It was a great way to say farewell and happy future to the Cunard Line!

The next day we were delayed getting off at our scheduled time due to the weather conditions. However, all went well and I disembarked at 5 p.m. Usually I disembark by 10 a.m. in New York. I had to call my limousine. It arrived at about 7 p.m. But it had been a wonderful trip and I was glad to finally be home!

Chapter Seven
Tours of London and Paris 1991

The year has rolled around and the time has come for what will be a banner year for me and all of my exploits of a sort. Since the last trip that I shared with you, the reader, life has been full to the brim with good things. I feel lucky, and never say that I wish for anything. Life seems to provide for all my needs as I go along.

I was deeply involved in the classes at Rutgers University. There wasn't a day that went by when I wasn't involved with music in one form or other. It was a way of life for me. I liked it all. There was the history of opera class with videos of the actual opera which we would discuss. There were tests to be taken. There was the opera workshop that was exciting. And there were the private vocal lessons every week with the best teacher in the whole world. At least that was the way I felt about her lessons. Thank you, Dr Schneider.

Then, of course, there were piano classes and more harmony study. The emphasis was mostly on jazz and improvisations.

Also, this year I attended the Penn State Reunion which I had not attended since I graduated. It was great to see my friends there. One friend asked me what I was doing. I replied by telling him that I was involved in playing the piano and singing some opera arias. He then asked me if I sang *Un Bel*

Di. I told him I had not. So, on my next year's agenda, believe me, I would learn to vocalize it.

Now, it was time to board my favorite ship, the *Queen Elizabeth II*. I would leave New York on July 9th, 1991. The morning was beautiful and warm. It would be good to see my *QE2* friends again. I arrived at the pier in a new pink suit. I was truly feeling in the pink. With me was no longer the one and only blue travel bag that I had when I began my travels. Now, there were three bags filled with exciting clothes to wear for sport activities and for day and evening wear.

The first day was spent walking around the deck, as usual, in the sunshine looking at the New York skyline. The ship seemed to be extra full of people on deck enjoying the beautiful weather. The schedule was much the same. We had our table placement. Again, I was seated at the doctor's table. This time it was Dr Eardley. Then we had the usual captain's cocktail party. It was festive as usual. I am always surprised to see so very many people attending. It doesn't seem possible there could be so many people cruising. Then we had the wonderful entertainers. Debbie McCormick, the dancer, came to greet me. She would be performing her dances with her husband again on this trip. It was pleasant to see her again. She was the dancer whose mother made her costumes. The evening followed the same format. There was a sparkling show to attend. Then my usual midnight buffet. It was the same as usual, but for me that is exactly what I liked!

It was nice to see friends from past trips. This trip, the Swedish officer who enjoyed the German translator some years ago was aboard with his Japanese wife and child. It is always a surprise to see old friends.

My cabin for this trip was 2010. This was fine for me. It was on the same deck as the Midships Lobby. That was where the white grand piano was located. I would have no trouble playing on it before going to my cabin at night!

So the five-day crossing went by. Now it was time for the talent show again. This show would be special because, for the first time, I had the courage to wear a long evening gown. I chose the long white satin gown. Then to complete the look, I wore a beautiful rhinestone tiara that I had bought especially for the *QE2* talent show.

If a singer was ever ready, I felt that this was the time! In the cabin I played my warm-up tape. Also, I knew exactly what to wear. Yes, I would wear the white satin gown that I loved and I would wear my beautiful new tiara. This was my special trip in many ways. I knew who my accompanist would be and he was excellent. He was Ashley Stanton. We had our rehearsal and I knew it would go well. Now there were three arias that I had music for that we would use if time and the audience seemed to want to hear them. They were a Giuseppe Verdi aria and two Giacomo Puccini arias.

After getting dressed, I went up to the Grand Lounge to sit in a chair by the stage. Now I was excited and felt like part of a real opera. People were gathering in the lounge to see the show. Finally, the show began with the rousing band playing *There's No Business Like Show Business*. The Master of Ceremony was Colin Parker. He was perfect. He made each contestant feel comfortable. It was my turn! It was great having a long gown; no one would know if my knees were shaking. This alone gave me confidence. Also, I was still wearing the ballet slippers. It was a nice combination with the tiered gown. Ashley played a few preliminary bars of music and then I sang. The aria was *Caro Nome*, by Puccini. It is a beautiful aria about a girl, Gilda, who is very much protected by her father. She is not allowed to go out except to attend church. At church she meets a young man with whom she falls in love. When she sings this aria, she is on the balcony of her home. *Caro Nome* means, of course, "Dear Name". The name of her love was Gualtier Malde. So she begins her aria by calling out his name. Then she tells about how her heart palpitates with the very thought of him. It is really a work of art from the composer Verdi.

I sang it with all my heart and Ashley Stanton accompanied me very nicely. Thank you, Ashley! My favorite audience clapped long and hard and I was thrilled. So it was that I followed with a Puccini aria, *O Mio Babbino Caro* and then, lo and behold, another Puccini aria, *Quando Me'n Vo*. The applause was great and it was a wonderful talent show!

Later that afternoon was time for appraisal. In my cabin, I prepared to hear the three arias on tape that I would have ready for my very special singing teacher at Rutgers University. However, to my disappointment, the batteries of the recorder had gone low and I could never retrieve that wonderful event again! Well, to be philosophical about it, the audience did enjoy it and that basically was the objective.

Arrival time in Southampton! While we waited for disembarkation we were asked to eat in the Princess Grill. It is what is called 'open seating'. It is a beautiful restaurant and I was glad to be seated there even if momentarily.

Arrival in Southampton was Sunday 14th July, 1991. The boat train was available for those wishing to go to London. So, onward, I proceeded to Waterloo Station. From there I took a London cab to the Grosvenor Victoria hotel. As you know by now, it is my favorite hotel. When I arrive in London my heart seems to skip a beat. London is so... London! There is no place to compare with it. Even though I was born in America, I often feel that London is really my home town.

Finally, in my room, I would make the calls to my brother and family in New Jersey. Then I would call my relatives in Mill Hill, on the outskirts of London.

My room at the Grosvenor was #234. If I should go there again I will ask for the same room. That is if you haven't taken it after I describe it. It was a lovely double room with chintz flowered drapes. It overlooked the park and the city streets. In the morning I could look out and see people hurrying to work. There was the park statue at the entrance of the park with an English hero seated on a horse. Apparently he was not killed in battle because all four feet of the horse are down. I understand that if the two front feet are raised, the rider was killed in battle. If one foot is raised, then he was wounded. So be it for the history lesson.

This day Elenora and her boyfriend from Mill Hill would come to see me. It was great to see them. We decided to take my favorite walking tour of London. That was the date with Big Ben. It was always my first priority when coming to London. We happily walked about. The city was very active near where President Bush was holding a summit conference. We, however, walked on to our target, Big Ben! We continued enjoying the day. We took pictures and then came upon a small clock-tower representation of Big Ben. Apparently it had been stored away for some time and then it was decided to use it. We took a picture of baby Big Ben!

The next day Eleanor and her mother and brother came to visit. They enjoyed a little lunch in the hotel and then we went to Mill Hill for a ride and dinner there. The weather was fine and we had a good time together.

I had booked a "Tale of Two Cities" tour of London and Paris with the Frames Coach Tours. This day, the 16th of July, I had to check in at the Bloomsbury Crest hotel. To get there I took a bus which was right outside of Victoria Station. It did take me to the Bloomsbury district but not to the hotel. It was a bit of a chore to carry my one bag. I had left the other bags behind at the Grosvenor until I would return. After inquiring at the post office, I was finally able to locate the Bloomsbury Crest hotel. There I would stay until it was time to commence the tour.

After a very fine continental breakfast, I met up with the tour that took us to see the changing of the guard at Buckingham Palace. For me, it was nice to be back in the area of the Grosvenor hotel. That was really my turf. Tomorrow I would need to get back to this area, on my own, to go to the Victoria coach station. This tour seemed to be a party of one!

We left the Bloomsbury Crest after three days of those good continental breakfasts. Now to wend my way to the Victoria coach station. Once there I got on board a bus for my trip to Paris. This would be an entirely different way to get to Paris. The last trip I had taken had been into Le Havre, France and then by train to Paris. I was looking forward to this trip. It was a relatively short trip that would take me to the hovercraft. We drove through the Kent countryside to Dover for the hovercraft crossing to France. The hovercraft was the big novelty. The inflated raft-like boat, of sorts, lifted itself by some kind of jet propulsion so that it rode over the top of the water. It was exciting! The noise from the engines made it seem more exciting! Whatever, I enjoyed that experience. We then arrived at the Continental Departure Lounge for a Hoverspeed City Sprint service to Paris.

We took the coach to Paris, occasionally stopping for a rest stop in the country. It was déjà vu all over again. I believe you know what I mean. However, we continued on to Paris and arrived in the late afternoon. After a rather sketchy way to meet with a representative who would take me to my hotel – I must mention again that apparently I was a party of one!

Anyhow, I found the meeting place, even though it was not easy. I wasn't even sure that the representative would actually be there. I did meet him and was put in a taxi to be taken to the hotel that was scheduled with the tour.

The hotel that I arrived at was Hotel France et Choiseul. My first impression was not good. They were doing some construction work and the entry was anything but inviting. I went in and showed my credentials and ticket from Frames Tours. I was then taken through some rather narrow halls to my room. The room consisted of one small cot-like bed. I was becoming more and more apprehensive. Was this a fire trap? It looked that way, but who was I to say. Whatever, I certainly was not pleased and would be thinking about ways to get out.

This particular trip was very special because a relative, Tara, would be in Paris also. She was attending La Maison d'Etudiants on Boulevard Ras Bail. We were to meet. It would give her some confidence although she was with a group of other students from America. Now I had to have a hotel that would be at least receptive to having her, if she needed to stay overnight. I knew the hotel I would like, even if I needed to pay extra for it. I had the Regina hotel in mind. It would be necessary for me to call Frames Tours to inquire.

It was now time for dinner. The Choiseul did not serve dinner. It was late. What to do? Necessity is the mother of invention. Evening though it was, I ventured out to look about for a place to have dinner. I hadn't gone far, when I saw an elegant hotel with people at dinner. In I went. I ordered. At this point, I had become a vegetarian. Either fashionable dining does not like this or there seems to be an air of needing to make special changes in the menu. To continue, the situation was resolved. I would get a platter of a combination of various vegetables that they had that day. Fine! My platter finally arrived. It was startling enough to look at. Indeed it was entirely vegetarian. However, what was taking up the entire center of the plate was a huge artichoke! I have never eaten them. Some people think they are quite a delicacy. I, however, don't like their pine-cone look. Consequently, my dinner consisted of eating the frugal veggies surrounded by this artichoke mountain. I was afraid to ask for what I really wanted, a good old-fashioned baked potato! The bill arrived. Forty dollars! I paid and went back to my inadequate hotel.

Early the next morning I made all the preparations possible for a change of hotels. The Frames people were very cooperative. I was allowed to change to the Regina hotel which I do like. Thereafter my bags were gathered and I walked the distance to the Regina hotel. It wasn't that close, but on the other hand, it wasn't that far away.

I arrived at the Regina hotel. What a world of difference! I was given a beautiful room which looked out over the city and with a magnificent view of the Eiffel Tower. It had a double bed and an exceptional bathroom that was huge and beautifully tiled. Yes, this was just the place for Tara. I asked the concierge if she could remain over night because we would be going to some of the evening entertainment theaters. He said it was all right. I was set to enjoy Paris.

On my first full day in Paris our Frames itinerary included a morning sight-seeing tour. It was easy to find the bus because it was directly across the street from my hotel. We saw the bridges over the Seine, the Opera House, the beautiful fountains, the famous Cathedral of Notre Dame, plus a close look at the Eiffel Tower. I went up to the first level to take pictures. In fact, I took so many pictures, that they didn't fit into the album.

Tara arrived in the afternoon after her classes at La Maison d'Etudiants. Then we made the most of our time together. We took pictures on the balcony overlooking the Eiffel Tower in the distance. We visited the Louvre and saw all of the famous paintings that we could. We took a barge through the canals.

In the evening we went to visit the Folies Bergere. There we had a splendid dinner. There were plenty of violinists to serenade us. The waiters wore white wigs, white socks and white gloves representative of the courtly days in France. They came down the central staircase carrying the silver platters of food to everyone seated at the long tables that were set up for the large number of guests.

The show at the Folies was very entertaining. It was also mighty expensive for admission and I paid for two! However, it was worth it. The acts were really enjoyable. We sat at a cozy small table to view the stage. Everyone seemed friendly and happy. The show lasted until the wee hours of the morning. However, there was no worry because we were escorted by a tour guide with the tickets we had bought in the tour office next to the Regina hotel.

On the last day in Paris, Tara and I shopped and went out for lunch in a quaint French café across the street from the hotel. We certainly did feel like Parisians, eating French cuisine and seated out doors in the sunshine with people passing by who we could look at as we ate. It was a great time together and I know it was well worth the trip and preparations to have the meeting there in Paris.

What was a trivial incident, that you would enjoy, was this. On that last trip to Paris in 1985, I noticed a grand piano in the lobby. At one point during my stay there I had time to sit at the piano to play. As I played, I was very much aware that the piano was most definitely out of tune. I did the best I could with it. Finally, I went to the concierge and told him about the piano being out of tune. He told me that the piano was never really played. There was no pianist that played there. Well I told him, "I hope that the next time I visit it will be in tune."

Now, there I was six years later and I saw the piano in the lobby. It was the same piano. Naturally, I went over to play the beautiful instrument. It was a cherry wood grand piano. I sat down to play it and would you believe it, it was still out of tune! The concierge at the desk was a different person, of course, but I told him the story and he just mumbled something in French. This time I did not say that I would be coming back to check on the "health" of the lovely piano. However, I often think about it and feel sad to know of an instrument that is not being taken care of properly. Vive la musique!

We said our farewells. In the morning, Tara went back to school and I began my journey back to London.

I started the journey back at noon. The Hoverspeed coach met with the tour passengers. They had come from other hotels they had scheduled for their stay. We traveled through northern France.

We made some stops along the way as was usual. Our destination was Calais. There we would meet up with the hovercraft. We would board the craft on our way to Dover, England. Then we boarded the Hoverspeed bus and drove back to London. We arrived at the Victoria coach station at 7.30 p.m.

Back in London and again in the Grosvenor Victoria hotel, I made preparations for a cruise down the Thames. I had not been on the Thames and was looking forward to doing so. It was good to be walking in London again. I walked to the ticket office by the bridge that spans the Thames. With ticket in hand, I boarded a comfortable all-weather boat at Westminster pier. It was a lovely day and the trip was relaxing and interesting. I enjoyed the on-board commentary.

If that was not enough for the day, I took a sightseeing bus. Never would I miss that ride through London. Of course, sitting on the upper level was the fascinating part. I could take all of the photos that I wanted. Also, one could learn about the history of the city by putting on the headphones. On other occasions, popular music was played, which made for pleasant listening as well as the visual pleasures.

In the evening, now back in my London hotel, my relatives in Mill Hill came to take me to the theater. I do like the London stage plays. We went to see *The Rose Tattoo*. It was entertaining and a way to spend the evening together. Florrie had driven into London in her car. However, on a lovely summer evening we were able to walk to the theater district. For some reason, London looks very safe. I would not go out alone, however. Since I was with a person who was knowledgeable about the city, I did not mind.

On my last morning in London, I went to pick up some pictures at Boots drug store. It was my favorite place to have my film developed. It was always a pleasant walk there from the hotel. Also, I went to the upper level of Victoria station. There I did some last minute shopping for gifts for friends back home. It was so convenient. It was literally at the back door of the Grosvenor Victoria.

Back in my lovely hotel room, I gathered my belongings. I then went to the baggage department to pick up the suitcases that they had stored there for me. I paid my bills and left reluctantly for Waterloo station. A cab outside the hotel took me to my destination.

The boat train was a very convenient form of transportation to Southampton. This train no longer exists. Other provisions must be made to get to Southampton. I had to be on time for the embarkation at 1 p.m.

I arrived at the pier in Southampton and saw the wonderful *QE2* in dock. People were approaching. One person I recognized was Ashley Stanton. He had been my accompanist on the eastward bound trip to Southampton. I was glad to know that he would be aboard because he accompanied me so well. Yes, I was beginning to feel the excitement of getting aboard!

The entire process of boarding a great super liner like the *Queen Elizabeth II* is part of the excitement of travel. We are assured of the departing time. It is an enjoyable procedure to saunter up to the ticket agents with passport in hand. It is often a pier that will have a music ensemble to accompany your walk up the gangway. It is great to be met at the Midships Lobby by a smiling hostess. In my case, it might be Elaine Mackay. She is such an integral part of the ship that she would be missed if she were not there to receive us. Thank you, Elaine!

Then I go down the familiar corridors in search of the cabin reserved for this particular journey. I have always been satisfied with my cabin on all decks and find that they have all been restful and easily accessible. There is an abundance of elevators to get you to any part of the ship. What I write seems to be a promotion for the ship. It is not. I am simply a very satisfied passenger. That is why, I guess, I have been taking the transatlantic crossings both east and west bound. They were during the summer and included the cruise that follows the transatlantic crossings.

Upon my arrival, I made some preliminary adjustments, which included finding my restaurant table and table number. This was usually issued to you on a card, to be found on your cabin dresser. It needed however, to be checked by the Maître d' and any adjustments that needed to be made were done at that time. I had completed all of that and now was the time to take my usual walk around the ship. This day, in the Grand Lounge, a high school band was giving a concert for the passengers. They sounded very good. I stayed to enjoy the music. At intermission time, a girl who I had noticed playing the cymbals sat next to me. We had a chance to talk a bit together. She told me where the band had come from in

England. She also told me that she liked playing the cymbals in the band because they were taught not only to play, but also how to twirl and flourish the cymbals over their head and about in synchrony with music. Yes, I had noticed! When we finally prepared to leave the pier that day, I went out on deck. There on the pier the band was in formation ready to play for us, which they did. The music was rousing and done with their fine flourish. I could see my new found friend making her flourishes happily. Then, a moment I will not forget, she spied me on the deck, high above her, listening to the music, then with a sign of acknowledgment, she raised her hand to wave to me. I waved back! It was the best send off I believe anyone could possibly have. Good luck to the cymbal player, wherever you may be! Thank you!

We were now on our way to cross the Atlantic. Captain Robin Woodall and his ship's company were aboard. This would be the 798th voyage. We would leave Southampton at 3 p.m. and arrive at Cherbourg, France, simply to take on some more passengers. Then about 10.30 p.m. we would be on our way to New York. We would arrive there on the 29th of July. So we had five wonderful traveling days ahead. Aboard would also be some of the usual crew that I was now used to seeing. They were Peter Longley, cruise director, and Lindsay Frost, deputy director and Elaine Mackay, social directress.

My table for this crossing was the doctor's table. That was always nice especially when it was his turn to sit at our table with us. Also at the table were a German couple and a couple from California. They were interesting to converse with at dinner in the evening. However, very often, I would either eat on deck or at the Lido, cafeteria style. In the Lido, there were two cozy places that I liked. From either place, I could enjoy my lunch in comfort and quiet, on the soft padded bench seats.

It was so cozy that I looked forward to eating lunch there every day.

The first day at sea, of course, we had the usual boat drill. This is an important procedure. Also, after that there was a lecture on traveling solo. This I did not attend. As I mentioned before, I preferred to find my own way about. However, I do think they are helpful for those who seek this information. Whatever, I was surprised to find on the schedule that a formal dress was requested for the evening. Since it would be the captain's cocktail party, there would also be a dinner dance in the Columbia restaurant. Since I enjoy dressing in formal attire, I was eager to get ready for party time. It turned out to be a lovely affair. I wore an ankle-length dress that was pink. I had the opportunity to dance and I had a good time.

If you are lucky, you might get an invitation to visit the bridge. In general, men like very much to have this opportunity. However, I found myself interested in knowing how the Queen of the Seas is driven. The bridge is situated at the forward end of the signal deck. It is an enclosed wheelhouse with navigational equipment. Behind the wheelhouse is a chartroom for charts and publications. The officers of the watch operate from the wheelhouse. The bridge is manned twenty-four hours a day. There is a first officer there and a second officer. There are three watches. I was surprised to see the driving wheel was so small. I don't know the exact circumference. It was smaller than I would imagine for such a huge ship. The gross tonnage is 66,450.63 and the net tonnage is 39,881.73. The overall length is 963 feet. The ship was built by the Upper Clyde Shipbuilders. However, the diesel engines were built by MAN, Augsburg, West Germany. There was so much technical information to learn that a passenger would be hard-pressed to remember it or understand its significance. It was a great privilege to see the bridge and I did appreciate it. Thank you!

The return trip was, in general, much the same as I have mentioned for other trips. However, there are always highlights to each sailing. On this trip, I enjoyed hearing the cruise director present in the theater "An Irish Garden Grows". He showed beautiful slides of heavenly gardens and told of design, creation and maintenance of twenty-five acres of gardens in Ireland. It was a position he had formerly had with an Irish family. I found that presentation very interesting. Thank you, Peter.

The other great part of the trip was the music. For this trip, we had a great band leader, Mark Joyce. He is not only a band leader, but also an excellent percussionist. Also, on this trip I heard Christine Trevett. She is a remarkable songstress. Together with the Mark Joyce Showband she was a terrific hit! I feel lucky to be aboard when they are also aboard to entertain. Thank you, Christine and Mark!

Actually, what I was looking forward to most of all was the up coming talent show. I recalled the eastbound show in which I had sung three arias! It was such a success with the audience clapping for more. Result: the three arias. However, as you know, my recorder happened to have a low battery. I had no way of preserving what I think, to this day, was my very best! Now, on this westbound voyage, I was not sure what would take place. Sometimes there are too many acts to have three songs to sing. As it happened, I sang two arias on this homeward trip. I made the usual preparations. I wore the white satin gown with the tiara. My accompanist would be Ashley Stanton. I was ready. Since the low battery episode, I had bought new batteries. Now, before writing I listened to the tape made at the time. It was a good recording. My voice was in great shape. I truly enjoyed listening to myself. The audience was also wonderful. They applauded vigorously and topped it with some ever-loving whistles! The talent show had been worth the wait. However, I will always miss the tape that didn't record. The sound effects engineer told me that he would have taped my singing if I had asked him to do so. However, I still use my recorder but I make sure the batteries are okay.

That evening, as I was still wearing my singing gown, two gentlemen from Stockholm came to me to tell me how very much they liked my singing. One of the men was a conductor and the other a concert pianist. They were so appreciative and it pleased me very much. The concert pianist said he wished he could have accompanied me. After I arrived home I received a large envelope from Stockholm. It contained a picture of the conductor and a letter from the concert pianist telling me again that they enjoyed my singing. If they had the opportunity again the pianist would play for me. It was my first "fan mail". Thank you very much!

The great trip was now over but the memories linger on and on. Before completing the trip there are two other memories I failed to mention. One was the lovely oil painting exhibit in the Midships Lobby by Peter Longley. He had some lovely florals of the Irish gardens that he tended before being a cruise director. I enjoyed the paintings very much Peter.

The other memory was that of listening to Greg Daikun playing the piano in and about the ship. As you know, my brother is an accomplished pianist. He plays jazz, popular or the classics equally well. Greg was from Canada. He had blue eyes that sparkled as he played. I warned him that "I fall in love with piano players." He was a good sport and enjoyed the comment. Good luck to you Greg!

That's it for the voyage of 1991. It was a very good year!

Rehearsing with Colin Brown – 1989.

A royal welcome for Cunard's 150th Anniversary – 1990, hip, hip, hip, hooray!

Singing *Caro Nome, Quando Me'n Vo* and *O Mio Babbino Caro*.

In the receiving line wearing the white satin gown for the Queens Room Ball – 1990.

Picture taken after singing *Caro Nome*. Note the tape recorder.

Singing *Caro Nome* and *O Mio Babbino Caro* in the formal white gown. Accompanist : Ashley Stanton – 1991.

No, I hadn't been seeing double. They are the Luke Twins!

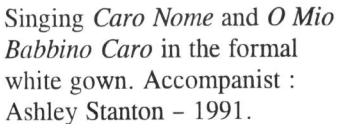

Return trip: Singing *Il Bacio* (The Kiss). Note the opera pearls.

Chapter Eight
Caribbean Cruise 1992

Welcome Aboard! This would be my first, or maiden voyage I would make to these southern waters of the Caribbean. My trips are always transatlantic. This would be an extra treat voyage! I was not looking forward to it as much as I had looked forward to other trips. However, it would be interesting to see what the vacationers' paradise was like.

It was early in spring that the cruise started, 14th April, 1992. The captain aboard was Captain Ronald Warwick. This was my first cruise with this captain. We would be visiting Port Everglades, St Thomas, Martinique, Barbados and St Martin. The itinerary was exciting as an extra special treat. I would not eliminate the usual transatlantic crossing during the summer months.

It was like a homecoming to go to the cabin and find a lovely bouquet of flowers from the travel agent and a bowl of fruit from the ship! After checking out the cabin, my steps hurried to get on deck. There was the familiar New York skyline and a visibly crowded deck of sun worshipers ready for the first rays of the year, warm enough to be outdoors and enjoy. The passengers seemed a bit different. There seemed to be more people from the New York area taking a break from office work or college students on spring break. I fell into the second category.

This year at Rutgers, since the last trip, had been spent on the usual music classes etc. However, the main emphasis was on vocalizing in preparation for the *QE2*. The aria I was working on was Puccini's *Un Bel Di Vedremo*, "One Beautiful Day is Coming". It is a beautiful aria from the opera *Madame Butterfly*. It is the aria that my colleague from Penn State asked if I could sing. With this intent, I worked at vocalizing each week during the year! In the meantime the opera workshop presented some great operas. My professor played the lead role. She had a great talent and I was always proud that she was my instructor. She presently teaches and performs in New York City.

On board were the usual good friends of the cruise office. They were Peter Longley, Colin Parker, Andrew Graham and Elaine Mackay. The first evening was informal because, of course, the unpacking and pressing of clothes might be necessary.

For the evening's entertainment a magician was scheduled. His name was Ward Thomas. I heard that he was also from New Jersey. However, I am not sure. Whatever, his act consisted of surprisingly presenting an abundance of colorful umbrellas seemingly from out of nowhere. I love this kind of magic. The kind that I don't like is when people are supposed to be sawed in half. I know it's an illusion, but nevertheless I don't like to see it. Umbrellas, birds or flowers from nowhere, yes. So, happily, began the cruise to the sun-drenched Caribbean!

After all of the preliminaries were complete, I began getting acquainted with the ship. There for the afternoon tea, I heard the sounds of *Moon River* being played by another pianist. Greg Daikun, from Canada, had not played that particular song. Now, hearing it, I decided to give the pianist a greeting. Usually pianists have a rather lonely art. They are sometimes overlooked in a sea of rollicking good cheer. I spoke to him by telling him that I enjoyed hearing *Moon River* being played and being played so nicely. I knew that immediately we became friends. Then since he was scheduled to entertain in the Yacht Club before dinner, I went there to hear him play. His name was Keith Ansell. There listening to him, I was reminded often of my brother who played the same songs. Then, if there was a special one that would remind me of home, Keith would kindly play it for me. Already I was beginning to feel glad that I had made the trip!

It so happened that the day before leaving for this Caribbean trip, I received a letter from the lady who had met her husband on a trip a few years ago that I wrote about. She mentioned that she would be taking a Caribbean trip with her husband. It happened to be at the same time that I was taking this trip. She, of course, did not know that! It would be quite a surprise for them to see me aboard. I didn't inquire about them when I boarded. I wanted it to be a chance surprise. Well, the time came as I entered the Yacht Club to hear Keith play the piano. She was seated with her husband amidst a group of happy mutual friends and party balloons! It was a happy sight. Instead of going to them immediately, I went to Keith and told him to watch when they would see me. So, walking slowly around the happy table, Doreen caught my eye. She jumped up to give hugs of surprise. I then found myself part of the party! This happens to be one of the rewards of travel and the friends you meet along the way. It is always a pleasant coincidence.

There was still time for moments for myself. Those were the moments when I would search out my piano in the Midships Lobby. One of the evenings that I was there, I happened to meet another piano player. He was obviously very talented. We talked about some classical compositions and which ones we liked. It was obvious that we were both involved in music.

It became known that he was a classical pianist who would be performing on the ship. He was concert pianist Francis Heilbut. It wouldn't be long before I would be practicing an aria with him, as the days went by, during the cruise, there in the lobby. We enjoyed the familiarity with the repertoire that we both knew.

Port Everglades was our port of call. This would be a childlike reference to the past when I was in geography class in grammar school. We found out then that the Everglades was a great expanse of swamp area in which lived colorful birds and alligators in high swamp grasses. It seemed exciting then. Now, after all these years, I would finally see this area and perhaps an alligator. My tour was to Everglades Safari Park. We arrived and boarded a boat to look for alligators to surface. To encourage them do so, the driver threw marshmallows into the swampy waters. I was ready to see one with my camera in hand. Well, I did get a lot of marshmallow pictures. However, I did get one picture of an alligator's eyes peering above the water about to retrieve a marshmallow. Success at last!

Our one small boat took us to the alligator museum of a sort. There the attendant showed us how he handled a large alligator. After that we were shown baby alligators. These little ones we were allowed to hold and have a picture taken. It was great fun for all!

The day in St Thomas was spent shopping. That was great, looking at all of the gorgeous jewelry and linens. I met Doreen and her husband in a jewelry shop. Remember the beautiful blue gems she had!

Easter Sunday. This would be the first time I had not shared Easter with my brother's family. On board, however, one could attend religious services of one's choice. For that day, I had reserved tickets to go to the flower gardens. There on Martinique were the Balata Tropical Botanical Gardens. It would be a heaven for photos. It surely was just that. The tropical flowers were splendid. I was amazed at the size of some of the plants and flowers. It was an extremely hot sunny day and I was able to use a *QE2* umbrella that I had received from a talent show, to shade myself from the sun! Thank you *QE2* for the umbrella. It is handy for both rain and sun!

Hopping between the islands in the daytime, there was also time at night for playing the piano and visiting the Yacht Club. I can't get enough of the piano sound. I follow it like following the Pied Piper! Keith knew I had studied French and I had studied singing the beautiful French song *La Vie En Rose*. It was the only French song that I had in my repertoire. Keith invited me to sing it in the Yacht Club. The passengers were relaxing in the club near the gorgeous white Lucite Shimmel piano. They enjoyed the bit of entertainment. Of course, I just happened to be wearing my rose-patterned chintz ankle length dress. It was a happy bit of French ambiance for the Yacht Club. Thank you, Keith!

For classical entertainment at 10 p.m. that Easter Sunday was a special piano recital featuring Francis Heilbut. Since I had met him practicing, in the Midships Lobby, I was anxious to hear him perform. He would be playing Beethoven's Moonlight Sonata, all three movements. It was a joy to hear him perform. His music had great depth and expression. It was another fine performance of the sort that one is able to get on the *QE2*.

One afternoon, Elaine Mackay had had her usual craft class. This having been Easter week, all those who joined the class were given a large straw sun hat. For this hat we were shown how to make flowers from crêpe paper. When the flowers were made, we attached them to the band of the hat. Then some pink ribbon was tied into a bow and the ribbon was placed in the back of the brim to hang down as an Easter spring-like decoration. It kept me from missing family on this special day. In the evening an Easter Parade was held for those who cared to show their hats. The schedule read as follows, "Don your Easter Bonnet with all the frills upon it and be the grandest person in the 'Easter Parade'."

The next day we gladly arrived in Barbados. It is the most easterly of the Caribbean Islands. Though just twenty-one miles by fourteen miles, its shores are what is called lavish with about sixty miles of glistening white sandy beaches. I did not go to the Carlisle Bay Center to swim. Instead, I chose a tour to see the Flower Forest. As the name suggests, it was truly a forest of flowers. To name a few for flower lovers, there were impressive stands of bamboo. There were double pink bougainvilleas, a red-leafed Heliconia, a Powder Puff Tree and pink and white begonias. There were two cabbage palm trees. The path led on and on. It was really a magnificent tour.

Tuesday the 21st of April. A telegram was sent to Buckingham Palace, in London. It was the occasion of Her Majesty's Birthday. We, however, went about with our tours. We had arrived at St Martin at 8 a.m. The first launch went ashore at 8 a.m. I did not take a tour. I wanted to look around the city and perhaps buy some trinkets. It is a happy place to window shop and enjoy the leisurely ambiance. I bought a few bits of trivia. There I met up with the piano recitalist, Francis Heilbut. We sang an aria duet in the expansive mall center. He said he would accompany me in the talent show. He needed to have permission to play for me. I appreciated that. Thank you, Francis! In the evening he performed again in the theater. He had a different repertoire. I enjoyed it.

Preparing for the talent show was a bit special. This time, after a year of preparation at Rutgers, I would sing the main aria for a soprano from the opera *Madame Butterfly*. It was for me a very exciting moment. Wearing the white satin gown reserved for the *QE2*, my recorder in hand, I sat by the stage to wait for the show to begin. The MC would be Colin Parker. He was such an excellent Master of Ceremonies. I was ready. I found the other acts very nice. I am pleased to listen and clap for each one while waiting for my turn. Finally, the time came when I was introduced: "A lady from New Jersey is here to sing opera for you." I went up a few steps to the stage and positioned myself in front of the microphone. I have had microphones that slipped or were placed too high for me. Now, I had the confidence to adjust it to suit my needs. Also I was feeling comfortable with the audience. They seemed like friends; all of them. Colin introduced me and announced what I would be singing; *Caro Nome*, a special favorite of my brother Michael and *Un Bel Di*. I had told the audience that I had a recorder with me because they were part of my performance when they clapped! I sang the first aria and then I told the audience that *Un Bel Di* was a premier performance! I sang it! I received a lot of clapping and a whistle. I also thanked Francis Heilbut for accompanying me. He received a lot of applause also. All of which was very gratifying. And, lest I forget, I received a *QE2* red umbrella which I had come to appreciate very much. I knew that Dr Jacklyn Schneider would get this one for doing such a good job of preparing me to sing such a difficult aria. Thank you Jacklyn, Francis, Colin and passengers!

It was quite a surprise that when at my dinner table I was presented with a bouquet of flowers. I really did feel like an opera star. Francis also received a bouquet of flowers at his table. I concluded that we were a success! Oh, such sweet memories! Later, I had a picture taken with the lovely bouquet of flowers so as never to forget the performance.

Now it was time to relax and enjoy the shows of the evening. They were always a good selection of different talents. This evening they had a comedian and a dance team. Then, my usual trip to the Yacht Club to hear the best popular player this side of heaven. That evening I wrote down the names of the songs that he played.

They were: *Memories of You, Small Hotel, People Will Say We're in Love, Long Ago and Far Away* and *Don't Make My Brown Eyes Blue*. Sitting at the white piano bar's grand piano was a delight worth a year of work and struggle. Keith played well and was a charismatic entertainer. I would be back!

The last port before New York was Port Everglades. Then we were on our way back to New York. With my Easter Bonnet on my head and carrying the red umbrella, I disembarked and took the waiting limousine back home!

This year, the coming back home meant preparing for another trip. The trip I mean was the upcoming transatlantic voyage. I had a lot of preparing to do. The preparing involved one aria. That was *Un Bel Di*. As you know, I sang it for the first time on the Caribbean cruise. Now that I knew it would be part of my permanent repertoire, I needed a gown representative of a beautiful spring day in a flower-filled garden in Japan. To this end I searched for the perfect gown to wear. There was a shop in New Jersey that had what I thought were the most beautiful gowns. After all I had bought my beautiful white satin gown there. Now I would look for another gown that would complete my feelings for the aria.

Expectantly, I went to the dress shop. There, sure enough, I found a beautiful light pink gown. It was very much the right shade of spring blossom pink! It had a full skirt of exquisite fabric, the back of which had a large bow that was shaped like a butterfly. The top was of pink sequins held by two narrow shoulder ribbons. It was lovely. Yes, it did fit me perfectly. It was a happy moment to walk out with my purchase.

As the days went by I started another search, for the proper fan! A Japanese girl must have a fan to sing this aria. So that quest began. Not any fan would do for me. No, I wanted a very special fan. Finally, after much searching, I came upon an art center featuring an artist who would match a fan to the color of my gown. This would be perfect! So she personally made one for me right there in the store. The basic structure she had. She added the appropriate matching material to it and put a bit of matching lace at the top portion. It turned out just to my liking. Now, what kind of headpiece would I wear? Well, it seemed that a wreath of small pink roses would be just what I needed to complete the special effect. So with that idea in mind, I decided to ask about having a rose-bud crown wreath made. This she also made to the right specifications and color. Now, I was ready for my transatlantic voyage!

Not quite! How about a video? Yes, I needed a video. Then I could not only hear but also see myself perform. Then I could really appraise my performance. Off to town to buy the video. I bought a Palmcorder Image. It is small enough to be held in one's hand and it takes great pictures. I practiced using it and found that it would be just what I could use on the trip. Now I was really ready!

It was the 5th of July, 1992. This was the beginning of a second trip of the year. It was a good year for travel. This time I would be going on my favorite transatlantic voyage. This trip was special because I was going to the famous Ritz of London. There I was to spend five days which included breakfast! It was a promotion made available by the Cunard Line. I felt that now I had made it in life, to travel and have reservations in this prestigious hotel.

After saying goodbye to my brother Michael and family and with visions of the Ritz in mind, I stepped into the stretch limousine. This would take me to the pier in New York. Now, sitting in the deluxe white limo, and talking to the Pakistani driver, it was again a thrill to be going on my summer *QE2* trip. Travel is one of life's joys.

The captain on board was Captain Robin Woodall. I liked that! Also aboard were the cruise staff that I knew. They were Peter Longley, Lindsay Frost, Herb Kritz and Maureen Ryan. The entertainers I also knew. They were the Mark Joyce Showband and Christine Trevett, songstress. Also there were the dancers Steve and Debbie McCormick. Also aboard was Keith Ansell at the piano in the Yacht Club. With Captain Woodall and those wonderful entertainers aboard, it was destined to be a fine trip!

Again, for this trip I was seated in the Columbia restaurant. This was my favorite one. It was where the silver loving cup was on display! At my table was a congenial group. Peter Longley, cruise director and others. One of whom was an actor from the Mystery Group. The theme of the voyage was a Murder Mystery presented by actors from New York. For five days the actors would concoct a maze of clues from a web of supposed murders. It added excitement to the voyage!

Now it was time to enjoy the after-dinner functions. For me the fun was to select the appropriate gown to wear. This I easily recall. The first formal night I wore a long pink gown that sparkled in the night lights. It was the night that I took my first video of Keith Ansell at the piano, with his permission. It came out beautifully. Now I could be at home and listen to *QE2* entertainment. The next night I wore the black and white ankle-length dress and attended a Mystery Night presentation. Then for Captain Robin Woodall's cocktail party I wore the long rose gown with the white flounce top! Yes, the pleasure of the occasion was partly the opportunity to dress in formal attire!

However, what was really on my mind was singing in the talent show. It had come to the point where I would be asked, when I embarked, if I would sing. I never did really know if I would. For some reason, I made the real decision to do so on the last day of the trip. I never even mentioned anything about participating to my dining table people. Some consequently didn't see me or were surprised when they found out about it.

Now it was the moment of truth. I signed up to participate in the talent show. I had rehearsed with the accompanist Ashley Stanton. I was dressed in the new gown, with fan and rose crown. Now, I needed to sing in my sweetest and best voice!

Colin Parker introduced me nicely. So well, in fact, that I would have liked to have recorded it. However, there was so much to think about! I had also given a passenger my camcorder to record the performance. Whatever, I introduced the aria that I would sing. As you know, it was *Un Bel Di Vedremo*. I sang it as beautifully as I could. Ashley put a lot of fortissimo into his accompaniment. The outcome was lots and lots of applause. Two waves of applause! It was really a wonderful feeling to please my favorite audience. Colin Parker, the MC presented me with a red *QE2* umbrella. Thank you Ashley and thank you Colin!

This is the best part. Captain Woodall's wife was also aboard. She met me at the World Club cocktail party. As I walked in with other passengers she introduced me as "The *QE2* Diva". This I will never forget. As you see now, how much this meant to me. It became the title of this book that I present to you, the passengers of the *QE2* who know me or have heard me sing. Now I would really continue to study vocalizing at Rutgers University with the memory of this trip. The Director of the opera department at Rutgers is a Valerie

Goodall. Now I can say: thank you Mrs Woodall and thank you Dr Goodall!

Onward! Into the Yacht Club to say goodbye to the piano player, Keith Ansell. Then I went to pack my bags and put them in the hall to be picked up for the next day's disembarkation. It would be an exciting day. I was going to the London Ritz.

The next morning, after a good breakfast, I waited for the call to disembark. When the call did come, I found that all arrangements had been made to have me transported by special bus. This bus would take us directly to the Ritz hotel. Along the way we were offered inviting snacks to make the trip pleasant. When I arrived at the Ritz, I was greeted by a friendly English doorman wearing a blue top hat. I was helped with my luggage into the hotel. There I had a lovely room with a lovely tiled bath. Later that evening I went down to dinner. I had a light vegetarian dinner. It was truly a simply divine hotel. I took a video picture of it. I could not believe that I was there and in London as well!

The next morning I was up and about at 7 a.m. I realized that during the night I had dreamed of Keith Ansell at the piano playing his music. It was no surprise because I had gone to hear him play each night. I guess my mind was still on the *QE2*. It had not left. My goodness!

I ordered a full breakfast to be served in my room. It was full service of all of the breakfast goodies. I enjoyed it. It surely was much better than staying at home and making my own breakfast! After breakfast I started out on the town. The weather was just a bit rainy but I loved it under my *QE2* umbrella. I went to have my films developed. It probably was at Boots, the drug store. Whatever, it happened to be the day the Serbian Parade was being held. It was an endless parade. I don't believe that I saw the end of it. The afternoon went by in a twinkling.

My relatives called from Mill Hill. We arranged a meeting to see a play and have dinner. It was always nice to meet family when so far away from home. We went to the Garrick theater to see the play *Dancing at Lughnasa*. It set me in a good mood for the nine days that I would be spending in London.

Then, one afternoon I saw a matinée performance of *Miss Saigon* at the Drury Lane theater. It was supposed to have a theme similar to *Madame Butterfly*. The theater was within walking distance of the Ritz. I didn't mind going to the theater in the daytime. However, in the evening, I stayed indoors preferring to have dinner in the hotel. Traveling solo is very nice but one must not take chances!

Another fine day, and they were fine days, because I was never hampered by inclement weather. I went to Windsor Castle with a local tour pass. I will never forget what a pleasant day that was. The castle was immense and imposing. The guides informed us of all of its historical past. Then the splendor of the day was highlighted by a parade of the palace guards. We lined the streets near the castle and simply immersed ourselves in the sheer excitement of seeing the men in their black helmets and red coats marching in precision down the street. Yes, this was London at its best. We all loved it!

Living near the shore in New Jersey, I had the desire to see a beach in England. The tour offered a trip to Boynton Beach. I decided to go. The trip there was relaxing. It felt like a holiday excursion, which it was in fact. I had taken a small lunch with me just in case I would be able to sit at the beach to watch the seagulls. Finally we arrived.

The bus let us off in the center of Boynton. There I had a chance to browse around the stores and look at what might be called a museum. It was a Middle Eastern looking building with many turrets and minarets. I do believe it belonged to a wealthy family at one time. However, I am not impressed by the inside of buildings. I prefer to be out in the sunshine.

With that in mind, I walked a few blocks in the direction of the beach. There it was. The stores with postcards on display were there, but where was the beach? I walked closer to where there was a boardwalk with several empty blue striped sunning chairs. From there I looked out towards the sea and... what was that? There the beach was totally covered with little brown pebbles. Amazing! How would one stand barefoot on those pebbles in the hot summer sun? That particular day, no one was out there. Also, no one was seated in the blue lounge chairs. Perhaps this was not the right time of day, I wondered. Then, I thought, it's those pebbles. Maybe the English don't like them either. Whatever, I looked and looked and then bought some cards and walked back to the bus. It certainly wasn't like my Jersey shore!

Florrie and her son Peter came to visit me the following day. We had tickets to see *Me and My Gal*. It was playing at the Adelphi theater. I was looking forward to seeing it because I had heard that the music was good as well as the outstanding British actors. Starring in it were Les Dennis, Louise English and Alfred Marks. It was directed by Mike Ockrent. I do very much like English theater. This musical was a special treat. Peter, who was about ten, was looking forward to seeing it also. My recollection of it at this time was that it was colorful and entertaining. It was to my taste. I preferred it to the show *Miss Saigon*.

The days were passing quickly. I had only five complimentary days at the Ritz. Now for the last four days, I would go to my usual favorite hotel, The Grosvenor Victoria near Victoria Station. There I would stay until the return trip on the *QE2*. I spent one of those days on a tour to Chartwell, the house where Winston Churchill resided. It was a wonderful estate. There were acres of beautifully landscaped gardens. It had a lovely quiet place where he could sit in his garden. It was near a small pool filled with goldfish swimming about. I liked that place and took several pictures of that area. A trip through the house was interesting as well.

The rest of the days, I busied about. Of course, I had my date with Big Ben. For that I could easily walk from the hotel to the clocktower near the park. There I would sit momentarily to hear the bells when they sounded. This is London, Mary!

Before leaving London, I went out to look for a rentable flat in the downtown area. There were some about a block away and to the left of the main road. I ventured out. To do this I had to pass a small fruit stand. I had often stopped there to buy a bag of delicious red cherries. I do like fruit. The cherries that I bought there made good traveling food. This day, as I passed, the friendly fruit vendor greeted me warmly, knowing that I would be buying my usual bag of cherries. Since I was leaving for home, I decided to tell him that this was my last day in London. With that news, he reached out and kissed my cheek! Goodness, these Englishmen! Love is such sweet sorrow!

Then there was enough time before leaving to take a sightseeing bus around London. It was a beautiful day. I sat aboard taking the names of all the popular songs that were being played. They were the classic popular tunes that I like so very much.

I also started taking pictures. A roll of film later, and I was ready to go and board the train to Southampton.

I did wish I could have gone to Southampton by bus, the way I had come as part of the complimentary reservation at The

Ritz. However, I went by train and arrived in Southampton to see the *QE2* waiting. Oh, what a beautiful sight!

Captain Robin Woodall would be our captain for this return trip. The cruise staff was much the same as the eastbound voyage. Also the Mark Joyce Showband would be aboard featuring Christine Trevett. The first night out a bon voyage party was held. That was an evening of fun, surprises and prizes.

The second night out to sea is formal night. It would be the Columbia restaurant's night to receive the invitation to the captain's cocktail party. I was happy to be back into a formal gown again. For this trip I had a new black gown to wear. It was a beautiful gown and I was looking forward to wearing it. At my table was the first engineer. His name was Nicholas Bates. We enjoyed having him at our table even though he came only for special evenings. That night he ordered Asti Spumanti. Thank you, Officer Bates!

Following the dinner it was another night of good entertainment. Then towards the end of the evening, I would again go to the midnight buffet. And, lastly, in the quiet of the Midships Lobby I sat down to play the piano. This was very relaxing for me. I had had a great time in London, but it was always nice to be back on the *QE2*.

Time was going along quickly. I was simply enjoying all of the great activities. The Grand Lounge had the music of Richard Rogers with the Mark Joyce Showband and Christine Trevett. The Jean Ann Ryan Singers and Dancers completed the bill. Later on I went to the Yacht Club to listen to the music of Keith Ansell at the piano. I told him that I had dreamed about him at the piano. He then asked me what song he was playing. I didn't know; it seemed to have been in silent film!

After premier performance of *Un Bel Di Vedremo* – 1992 Caribbean Cruise. Accompanist Francis Heibut, concert pianist.

Captain Woodall and I in his receiving line.

Wearing the new gown, fan and rose tiara for the *Madame Butterfly* aria.

Great applause for Ashley Stanton and I after the *Un Bel di* aria.

Colin Parker M.C. presenting me with a momento and a red QE2 umbrella.

Happy Birthday Julie! – 1993.

Richard Parker M.C., Captain John Burton Hall and I at the Captain's Passenger Party.

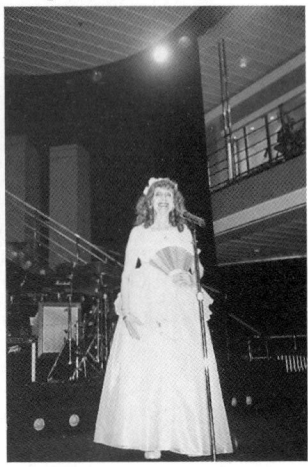

A high point, singing *Un Bel Di Vedremo* while at sea.

The last day and another talent show. Now I knew the aria would be *Un Bel Di Vedremo*. It was one that the captain and his wife would like because it was about a naval officer. I sang it and dedicated it to Captain Woodall. Ashley Stanton was the accompanist. Everything went well and I received a lot of applause. This I would tell to my singing teacher, Dr Jacklyn Schneider, at Rutgers University.

The travel for 1992 was now over and just a memory!

However, I was beginning a new fall term at Rutgers and a new aria for next year. This year I put a great deal of effort in with my teacher in learning the aria from *La Boheme* called *Si Mi Chiamino Mimi*. It is about a flower girl. I loved it. And yes, I bought a spring-green gown to wear and a basket with artificial flowers. It was so beautiful I couldn't wait to sing it on my next trip on the *QE2*!

Chapter Nine
World Cruise, Last Segment 1993

It had been slowly coming upon me, the urge to go around the world on the *QE2*. I now began looking at the itinerary for just such a trip. Also, for each port that the *QE2* was scheduled to visit, I would look up in the library what I might see at that port. This year the *QE2* had a segment of the world cruise that it would be possible for me to take. The year of 1993, the ship's itinerary indicated that part of the world cruise would be returning to New York to complete the last portion of the cruise. That meant I could board in New York and go to Greece, Morocco, etc. I had never seen these countries and decided that this would be the trip for me to take. Along with this decision came the realization that if I traveled with another person sharing my room, the person could go at half fare. I decided to ask my brother Michael's daughter if she would like to go. She said, "Yes", she would like to go. Great! Since it was about the time of her birthday, I made an indication on the ticket to request a special cake in the restaurant to celebrate a birthday. It was a fun expectation for both of us. This would be my first trip with a cabin mate! Welcome Julie!

We made arrangements for her to meet me in Southampton. She would fly and I would take the *QE2* on my usual transatlantic voyage. It would work out very well. We both looked forward to meeting on the *QE2*, where I would be waiting for her.

Departure time came for me that morning of 19th April, 1993. It was a rather dark cloudy morning. I was waiting for my limousine to arrive at 10.30 a.m. I was a bit apprehensive. I had never sailed to Europe at such an early time of the year. My trips were always in the summer. How would the sea be at this springtime? I had seen some lightning at about 6 a.m. when I awoke!

All aboard! It was reassuring to find that Captain Robin Woodall was in command. Also the cruise staff was much the same. It is nice to find friends aboard. The only update I get during the year about personnel aboard is from the social directress when she sends her newsletter at Christmas. Thank you, Elaine! Now I was again with friends and pianos.

The excitement of just being on a segment of the world cruise was beginning to brew. On schedule was an informal lecture by Waldemar Hansen, port lecturer. His subject was "Prelude to Majorca: George Sands and Frederic Chopin". The lecture was held at 10 a.m. in the theater. It was interesting to me because I do have Chopin compositions in my repertoire of classical pieces. He told the story about the winter Chopin and George Sands had spent at the Mallorcan Carthusian Monastery at Valldemosa. It was a romance that I had read about but enjoyed hearing about again.

My dining table was special. I had the privilege of sitting at the table with Elaine Mackay, the social directress extraordinaire, and her mother and aunt. It was such a nice compliment to be with them. I believe it may have been her mother's first trip accompanying her daughter. It was special for both of them.

In the evening we had our usual round of scheduled good entertainers. There was a multi-instrumentalist, Allan Randall. I enjoyed his music and the Mark Joyce Showband. There was also a hypnotist. This I did not attend. I just do not care for that type of entertainment. Also I did not go to the Yacht Club because Keith Ansell was not at the piano. However, I did go to the midnight buffet and played the piano in the Midships Lobby!

The next day aboard there was another lecture scheduled in the theater at 2.30 p.m. It was "Prelude to Corsica; in search of Napoleon Bonaparte". Napoleon was born in Corsica. He went on to live a spectacular life and die in exile on remote St Helena island. It was an historic hour of lecture and slides. It was great to learn or renew facts learned. Although it would be some time before the *QE2* would get to Corsica, it was something to look forward to seeing.

Also aboard was an art collection. The art director took those interested in art masterpieces on an art walk. I mention this to indicate the diversity of interest that the *QE2* has available for its passengers. I certainly enjoyed seeing the reproductions of the great paintings.

Time had come for the talent show. This past year I had worked on another aria with my voice teacher. The new aria that was now ready was *Si Mi Chiamino Mimi*. It is an aria from Puccini's *La Boheme*. It is a beautiful aria about a flower girl. It suited me just fine. However, I decided to wait until the talent show when my niece Julie was aboard. Then she could take a video and get a sound related picture to assess when I returned home.

Therefore for this crossing, I was still solo. So I chose to sing *Un Bel Di*. Fortunately, Ashley Stanton was on board to accompany me. He knew my repertoire and was always a fine accompanist. I wore the pink gown with fan and headpiece of flowers. It went very well. We received a lot of applause. Thank you, Ashley.

Upon arrival in the beautiful port of Southampton, those of us who were continuing on the world cruise had an opportunity to take a bus tour to the surrounding area. It is always a pleasure to visit the New Forest, Stonehenge and Salisbury with its spired cathedral. I enjoyed it. However, my mind was on seeing Julie. Incidentally, she was named after my mother, Julia. So, I waited for her to board in the Midships Lobby. While I waited, I played the piano. Finally I saw the familiar face! We were happy to see each other. I was glad she had made the transatlantic flight safely.

We went to our cabin #4179. There we unpacked her clothes and put them in the dresser drawers. Then we went up on deck to look about. On this voyage Captain John Burton-Hall would be in command of this 1993 World Cruise Mediterranean Odyssey. We would be calling at some of the most fascinating ports in Gibraltar, Majorca, Corsica, Italy, Greece, Sicily, Morocco, Portugal and then returning to Southampton. Now, with Julie and my video camera, it was going to be my most splendid of trips!

Since tomorrow we would be making our first port of call on Gibraltar, we went to a lecture. It was at 11.15 in the theater. Waldemar Hansen, port lecturer, was giving a lecture on "Bastions and Barbary Apes". I had seen the Barbary Apes, so Julie and I went shopping for gifts for the family at home.

In the evening was the special cocktail party given by the captain. It was another happy affair. I was again surprised by the number of people in attendance. This evening I had the opportunity to talk to the captain and with another favorite MC Richard Parker, brother of Colin Parker. I was able to get a picture of both of them. Thank you!

That same evening we had a celebration, at our table, of Julie's birthday. We had a nice table for four in the Columbia restaurant. We were seated with two other ladies from New York. They were good company. At the proper time after our meal, the waiter came to the table with a beautiful two-layered cake. On it was written "Happy Birthday Julie". The candles were lit and the waiters from far and near gathered around. Then everyone one sang "Happy Birthday". Everyone clapped and smiled in celebration. Cheers, Julie!

It was Sunday and we docked at North Mole, Gibraltar. We decided to take a taxi to the shopping area. Julie wanted to buy some Lladro ceramic figurines. We found a shop that sold them. There we spent a fun time just appreciating the art of the various figurines. We bought the ones that we liked. Then for the men in the family, for those special occasions, we went looking for the Monte Cristo #2 Cigars. We understood that they were very special and hard to find. The weather was perfect. It was a holiday just to walk about enjoying the happy people also enjoying shopping sprees of their own. A great day was over at about 5 p.m. The gangways were lifted and we set sail for Palma De Mallorca.

The weather seemed to have become a bit misty. At dinner the waiters were having trouble holding the dishes in their cupboards. We sat trying to enjoy dinner, then when things got really rocky we left. This happened to be the Bay of Palma that we were passing through on our way to Mallorca. Apparently the sea is often rough here because of shore currents. Since it was Julie's special trip I wanted the sea to be calm. In fact, it had been calm for most of my sailings. The social directress once said it was nice being on board when I was on board because the sea was always so calm! This time it was a bit rough. There was an announcement that we would not be able to disembark at Palma De Mallorca as planned. The sea was too rough for the launches. We were disappointed because we had promised everyone a string of the famous Mallorcan Pearls. What to do? What to do?

That night I shall never forget. In the middle of the night I heard various articles from my dresser scatter around the cabin floor. When I got up to retrieve them, I had the feeling of walking uphill to get to the dresser. Something was not right! Back in bed and I soon fell asleep. I guess I'm a good sailor!

The next day we passed Mallorca. I looked longingly at the shoreline and thought of all those pearls I had intended to buy! To make up for it I took video pictures of whatever I could see of Mallorca from a distance. I got plenty of those white caps bobbing around.

That same evening of the rough sea, we did have the opportunity to hear the very dynamic personality of Christine Trevett with the Mark Joyce Showband. I wanted Julie to hear her sing. She is by far my favorite singer. After listening to her, Julie was also a fan of her terrific singing style. Wherever you may be, applause to you Christine and Mark!

Bienvenue en Corse! Welcome to Corsica! The weather now was just fine. We took the early launch out to Ajaccio, Corsica. We wanted to do more shopping and looking. It so happened that an adorable blue mini-train operated from the port area. We decided to board it. The fare was reasonable. It took us past Ajaccio's highlights such as the Place de Gaullem the Napoleon grotto, and his monument and legendary "Rotts des Sanguinaires", returning along the narrow alleys of the Old Town past Napoleon's birthplace. The rest of the time we spent buying the pearls that we didn't get in Mallorca. Also I bought a small silver statue of Napoleon for my brother. The pearls were for his wife. We made up for what we had missed in Mallorca. We were two happy *QE2* tourists!

Benvenuti in Italia! Welcome to Italy! This was the country I was looking forward to seeing. I had taken a trip here with my parents. At that time it was on the Italian ships *Michelangelo* and *Raffaelo*. It would be exciting to see how much I could remember having seen. I knew that I would remember the port. It was there that we had our Cadillac taken off the ship so that we could drive around Europe! The charge to take the car aboard was the same price as that of a passenger ticket. Now, I would be looking at that same pier. Believe me it was a thrill.

We took the tour to Naples and Herculaneum. We knew, however, that we would have some time to shop. I wanted to see the beautiful Galleria in Naples. There, my mother had bought some jewelry. Now, I wanted to buy something for myself and Michael's wife. We were able to buy some cameos in a special store. I also bought an opera-length string of pearls.

Our tour bus took us for a drive around the city of Naples. I looked for places I remembered. We saw, of course, the towering landmark of Vesuvius, the "Old Man with His Pipe", as the volcano is sometimes called. We saw the very imposing Grand Castle Dell' Ovo, once a royal residence. We saw Castle St Elmo high on a hill overlooking the town. It was the former Carthusian Monastery. Now it is the National Museum of San Martino. We were then driven to the lower harbor area of the Via Partenope's grand hotels and picturesque waterfront restaurants facing the bay. This part of Naples brought back memories because I had stayed with my father, mother and brother, Michael, there at some of the hotels. We continued the road that winds upward to the Posillipo. Then we went to the Hill of Naples where we would reach the Vomero. There you had a spectacular view of the bay! We then returned to the central area of Naples. The San Carlo Opera Theater could not be overlooked in its grandeur. Then, of course, what I had wanted most to see, the wonderful cross-shaped arcades of that famous glass-domed galleria that I had seen with my parents. Julie and I were able to buy some jewelry there. It was great!

From Naples we were taken to Herculaneum. It is about seven miles from Naples. The bus driver made a stop for us at the cameo factory. There you could get any cameo of your choice of authentic quality for the most reasonable prices. We were delighted to delve about the showcases looking for what we liked. I bought a beautiful cameo pin and ring. Julia bought some cameos of her choice. We left happily!

Next we went to see the ruins of Herculaneum. It had suffered as Pompeii's sister city in disaster. Buried in volcanic mud, it took longer to excavate than Pompeii. Herculaneum's choice relics include mosaic in the House of Neptune and Amphitrite. The elaborate summer homes there were ornate with baths, kitchens and rooms elaborately painted. We saw evidence of where boats were docked at a shoreline that was there before the eruption. It was a most fascinating tour. The driver and tour guide did their very best to describe the situation. I was glad to be generous with my tip!

The time had come for me to premier my new aria that I had studied for the past year; *Si Mi Chiamino Mimi* from the opera *La Boheme* by Giacomo Puccini; "Yes, They Call Me Mimi." I truly loved the aria. For this reason, I will translate the words so that you get the beauty of the aria.

In the opera Mimi is introducing herself to another apartment dweller who has befriended her. This is what she sings:

> Yes, they call me Mimi. My story is brief. I sew and make paper flowers. It is tranquil to make lilies and roses. I like these things because they speak of sweetness and love, and springtime. They speak of dreams that have the name of "poetry". Do you understand? They call me Mimi. Why? I don't know. Alone I make my dinner in the evening. I don't go to mass but I always pray to the Lord. I live alone in a white bedroom. From my room I can see all of the roof tops touching the

sky. When the thaw comes, the first rays of sun are mine. The first kiss of the springtime is mine! The first sun is mine! There is a rose in a vase with real petals and thorns. How gentle is its perfume. But the flowers that I make, the flowers that I make (repeated), don't have any scent.

Then there is a little recitative added in somewhat of a spoken tone. "Other than what I have told you, I have nothing more to say except thank you for listening to me."
I made the above translation myself. It was a close recreation of what is indicated in the Italian lyrics. It is such a beautiful aria. I love it. Now I would be prepared to sing it to my friends on the *QE2*. For the occasion, I had bought a long green satin gown that I thought reminded me of springtime. With this dress I would carry a basket of paper flowers of lilies and roses. Then I would sing my very best!
The MC for the performance was Rudy Franklin. My accompanist was David Moore. I was in good singing form. The applause was great and rewarding. The best part is that this was the first time I had the complete performance on video. Julie took the video on my camcorder. It shows me giving a relaxed translation of the aria. It was spoken well and slowly for all to understand. Then I sang. It is such a lovely aria that it sounded perfect in every way. I am glad that I have the video. Thank you one and all!
At dinner, I received compliments from people seated near me on my singing. It is a good way to help digestion. I didn't tell the two people at my table. I had not gotten to that point of self-assurance that I could feel that I could announce the fact that I would sing. That would have to come later on future trips!

After dinner we enjoyed a show in the Grand Lounge. Featured that evening was an Adagio Dance Team. I think the Adagio dancing is exciting to watch. It isn't presented very often. I believe it gives the wrong impression of relationships! There were other performances that evening as well. The best of which was the music of the Mark Joyce Showband.

Welcome to Greece! I was looking forward to this. It was the land of the famous philosophers Socrates, Plato and Aristotle. My father had a library of philosophical books. It was the reason that my doctoral level was in philosophy. I enjoyed reading about the ancient Greek sages. Now, the tour we selected was Athens and the Acropolis. Since the *QE2* docked at 7 a.m., we would be departing at 9 a.m. We were docked in the port of Piraeus. It is a major Mediterranean harbor. From there we traveled by bus through the city of Piraeus to Athens. It was a gorgeous day. We saw all of the landmarks described by the bus tour lady as we went along. The commentary was very interesting. I had no idea that this area was so densely populated. It was more than I had ever expected. We finally arrived at the Acropolis. The classical sights came into view. Julie and I were ready with our camcorders to take all of the pictures that we could take. We saw the Parthenon's crowning beauty at the top of the Acropolis. There a *QE2* photographer spied us and took a picture of Julie and I together with a wonderful background of the Acropolis. We continued to take our own pictures. I liked the Erechtheum with its Porch of Maidens, that supported the portico. It was amazing to know that it was built in 421BC-406BC. There was so much to see. I marveled at the view of Athens and Piraeus from the Acropolis. The density of the cities from such a height was amazing. I couldn't take enough pictures of the view. The day that we were there, the tourists were there in crowds. Along with these groups were school children with their teachers out on field trips. I saw rows of the dearest children. It was such a pleasure to see them. Yes, I took pictures of them. It will be remembered as a wonderful day at the Acropolis!

Onward! Now the next port was Messina, Sicily. The ship docked at 1.30 p.m. We did not sign for a tour. Again, I preferred to stay in the port city. That day Julie was not feeling well, I went on my own. This was another city that I had visited with my parents and brother. I was excited to see if it would look the same. We had come last time with our Cadillac. We toured the entire island then. Now I walked to the Via Garibaldi, not far from the pier, where the brightly trimmed horses and carts were. I couldn't wait to take a ride in one of the carts. I would be alone, but it was daytime and surely it was safe. So I approached the cart driver to inquire about the price. He said it would be forty American dollars. I thought it was a fair price, so I accepted. There I sat, on a cart in Sicily, alone on the first day of May, 1993. It didn't matter, I was very happy. It was a beautiful day and this was the first cart ride in my life. It was a marvelous feeling! I tried speaking a little Italian to the cart driver. I had taken Italian courses for singing purposes and for travel. Now I was trying it out on Gaetano the driver. I told him that I wondered if the Cathedral of Bellini the composer, was located in Messina. I would have liked to have visited it. The conductor at Rutgers had made a visit there. He told me that he appreciated Bellini's operas so much that he had enjoyed making that visit to the birthplace of the composer. However, I realized it was Syracusa and not Messina. At least we were able to converse and understand each other. I decided to sing the first few bars of *Un Bel Di*. It was such a beautiful day and I had known that Italians like to sing while riding in the carts on beautiful days and evenings. It was really a happy thing to do. Gaetano complimented me with a "Brava, Brava"! I was able to get this serenade on my camcorder which I had taken with me on the ride. When I arrived home I viewed it and enjoyed it very much! Thank you for the cart ride, Gaetano!

After having driven to the town cathedral that dominated the city's landscape, the aquarium and other beautiful buildings, Gaetano had driven me back to the Via Garibaldi where the *QE2* was berthed. I had really enjoyed the ride and was sorry that Julie had not been there to enjoy it also. She had gone to the ship's doctor. He gave her some pills for the slight fever that she had. She gradually got better.

"Come with me to the casbah." We were now on passage to Tangier in Morocco. We spent the day enjoying cruise life. It was a Sunday so we went to the interdenominational service of morning worship. It was conducted by Captain John Burton-Hall. It was a fine presentation. After lunch we walked about and finally went at 2.30 p.m. to hear the travel lecturer, Waldemar Hansen, tell about Morocco and Tangier.

Our tour was to take us to Tangier, pronounced Tanjay, and to Cape Spartel. What I most wanted to see was a camel! A country that had camels walking about was what I expected. Tangier is the northernmost tip of Africa. It has a turbulent history. After years of changes by ruling countries, it became an integral part of Morocco. What I know is that I never felt the excitement on arriving in any country as I felt on going to and being in Tangier. It was simply a wonderful experience. The weather was ideal. The people were in their Moroccan dress. The men wore a fez and a flowing white djellabah. Children were everywhere. As I got off the bus a child offered me a field flower. I bought it with a quarter that I had in my purse. It wasn't long after that there was a crowd of little children around me. I knew that I had a lot of quarters so I put one in each of the little outstretched hands. The crowd began to get bigger. A man in a white djellabah came to my rescue and settled the situation. I will never forget the joy it was to give those children the coins. Yes, I really liked being in Tangier.

On our bus ride to the Cape Spartel, we saw beautiful homes. The tour driver said that many were owned by Americans. Occasionally, we stopped to get out of the bus. There we saw a camel that I had been waiting to take a close up picture. It was exciting until I heard it bray loudly. Then, oh, my, it smelled so badly I didn't want to get any closer. In the meantime a man in a djellabah was trying to sell me some jewelry. It was all in good spirit. However, I was waiting to go to the casbah! There we planned to go on a shopping spree. The casbah is the market place that is famous throughout the world.

We arrived at the casbah. Here we were deluged with Moroccans selling fezzes, pocketbooks, jewelry, djellabahs, etc. It wasn't easy avoiding some of the vendors. I bought a fez from a ten year old boy. He was so thrilled to make the sale. I bought a djellabah for my friend Larry. And, I bought my favorite souvenir, a small stuffed genuine leather camel!

At no time did the tour leader let the passengers out of his sphere of watchfulness. He was always ready to direct us to where to do some shopping. He told us that he would take us to a place where they sold carpets. He took us there. We all sat and watched the salesmen tell us about the fabric, color and hand-made products they had for sale. The tour leader urged us to bargain. Julie became interested in a lovely blue and white carpet about a medium size. There was an exchange of prices until the price was lowered to an acceptable amount. Sold! It was wrapped quickly, a handle attached to the cord and away we went. Julie smiled!

Last stop would be the home of Malcolm Forbes. It is a gorgeous palatial mansion done in blue and white tile. The

Moroccan-style mansion was situated on a hill overlooking the Mediterranean. The gardens were thriving with beautiful flowers in a symphony of colors. I was in seventh heaven! We lingered, took pictures galore, and then returned to our bus.

As I was getting on the bus another group of children gathered around me and another few coins were dispersed. Then as I got into my seat on the bus, I was aware of a vendor hastily showing his wares to me through the window. He kept it up. They were various articles of costume jewelry. The price kept getting lower and lower! Finally, out of appreciation for his grand performance, I bought a bracelet that matched a smashing Moroccan neckpiece that I had been pressured into buying earlier. Both pieces were encrusted with orange colored stones! The vendor waved happily as we drove away in our bus. It had been a beautiful and satisfying day!

It's wonderful being on a world cruise on the *QE2*. I do hope that I will some day be able to take the entire around the world voyage. For now, we were on our way to Lisbon. I had been to Lisbon before, as I have written. I do very much like the city. Also being with Julie, it was destined to be even more fun. I knew we would go on another shopping spree. That I knew she liked. The *QE2* docked at Alcantra Quay, Lisbon at 8 a.m. We were on an assigned tour bus at 9 a.m. We had with us a purse full of escudos to facilitate shopping. Off we went!

Lisbon is a beautiful city with many large open plazas. The center of these had a statue to a Portuguese hero. This was impressively placed in the center of the square. The hero was usually mounted on a horse. Around this area are beautifully mosaic-inlaid sidewalks. One of the centers called The Rossio was where Julie and I decided to use as our pivotal point to get back to our bus so that we wouldn't get lost. However, to continue with our tour, we were taken by the maritime quarter where there is a huge monument to Portuguese navigators. Also we saw the Tower of Belem, built in 1515. It was there that Vasco Da Gama set sail for India. We continued riding through the beautiful town, which is overlooked by the colossal Christ the king statue which looms 157 feet and weighs 40,000 tons, the arms of which are spread in benediction. We loved the sights but Julie kept her eyes on the department store windows. Eureka! She spotted a purse in a store window that she definitely wanted! I didn't think much of the tirade about how much she liked that bag. Later when we got off the bus at the square, she said she was going to buy that bag. I said, "Julie, how would you ever find that same street after all of the riding that we have done?" Her reply was that she had taken careful note of all the turns and twists of the ride and that she could find the store. I went with her, double checking the route along the way. Sure enough, we arrived at the store. There was the bag in the window! We went in and bought the prized item. Then after making even more purchases, we left happily and had no trouble finding our way back to the tour bus.

At 5.30 p.m. it was all aboard time. That was the nice part of cruise travel. At the end of a terrific shopping and touring day seeing unbelievable sights of past glory, it was nice to find a good warm meal and sociable friends!

That evening, besides good food and sociable people, on the agenda for entertainment in the Grand Lounge was proudly scheduled Petula Clark. We all love her rendition of *Downtown*. We have all heard her sing. Now, I would have the chance to see and hear her sing. What a great way to conclude a great day. We went to the lounge to hear her sing. She was just as endearing as you could imagine her. Among the songs that she sang was *La Vie En Rose*. It is a favorite of mine. I have done a good bit of study and vocalization with the number. She not only sang it but also accompanied herself on the piano. I didn't know that she provided her own accompaniment. Later that evening, we had an opportunity to meet. I told her how much I enjoyed hearing her sing *La Vie En Rose*. She said she also liked that number. Thank you for talking to me, Petula!

I must mention, this is another great aspect of travel. It is an opportunity to meet celebrities. How well I remember getting on the *QE2* for the first time and knowing that Regis Philbin, an American TV celebrity would also be on the ship at the same time as I was traveling. So it was another enjoyable evening aboard ship.

Now we were on passage to Southampton. This meant only one thing, Julie would be leaving to catch a plane to the USA. I would be traveling back by ship. We would meet in five days to talk about our joint holiday on the world cruise. All of her goodies were packed that last day. She had the purses, the pearls, the cameos, the cigars and the special presents she had bought.

The next day at the pier in Southampton we saw my pier lady, Elizabeth Taylor. We exchanged our usual good luck greetings! Then Julie boarded the bus for the airport with the other two table companions who happened to be going to the USA as well. See you, Julie!

At 2.30 p.m. the gangways were raised and shortly afterwards the *QE2* set sail for New York. It was a time to be back with friends again. Captain John Burton-Hall would continue in command. Lindsay Frost, Andrew Graham, Herb Kritz and Elaine Mackay were the social crew. Many passenger friends were also aboard. However, what pleased me most was that the piano player who played my brother's style of music and songs was also aboard. He was Keith Ansell. I would not feel alone when I heard his rendition of *I'm*

Getting Sentimental Over You and other favorites that he played.

The following day at sea was Sunday. It was my custom to attend the Interdenominational Divine Service of morning worship. It was conducted by Captain John Burton-Hall. I would follow this by a leisurely walk on deck. There I met a lawyer and his wife from Spring Lake, New Jersey. It is the same shore that I spend some summer vacations. It was interesting to talk to them because they knew some of my friends there.

At the table in the Columbia restaurant a German couple sat at our table for eight. They were from Chicago. During the conversation, the husband said that he would take a video of me singing in the talent show. It was always difficult to find someone who knew how to take video pictures. I was happy to know that he would do it for me. Thank you very much.

The day for the passenger talent show arrived. Since Ashley Stanton was aboard, I knew that I had a good accompanist. I decided to sing two arias. I wore the pink gown because it was the month of May, I wanted to convey the feeling of spring. With that in mind, I decided to sing the *Si Mi Chiamino Mimi* aria because I would be carrying flowers and singing about spring.

When my turn came, Rudy Franklin, the MC who knew me from previous voyages, knew exactly how to introduce me. I have taken my singing seriously and I do appreciate being introduced in the same vein. He did so nicely by saying that I had been studying music for four years at Rutgers University. All went well. I introduced my first aria by dedicating it to all of the mothers in the audience. It was Mother's Day, 10th May. The aria went well and it videoed perfectly. The next aria, *Un Bel Di*, I dedicated to Ashley Stanton because he seemed to like that aria. He was a good accompanist and I was glad to dedicate it to him. It went well also. Now I have a remembrance of the day. Other passengers may have taken a video also. Videos were becoming popular.

With the talent show over, so was my world cruise segment. I packed my suitcases and got ready to disembark. It is always a bit sad. However, I had visions of returning!

Chapter Ten
Norway and North Cape 1993

It's unbelievable! After that world cruise segment, I am now embarking on a trip to the North Cape! It is the same year, 1993. It is my usual summertime crossing vacation. I am really looking forward to the trip. It is the month of July. The weather is very hot in the States. It will be nice to be where it is cool.

It was a warm summer day when I left New York. I was wearing a white suit and white cotton blouse. I wore my happy smile because it was always a joy to board the wondrous ship. For me, the *QE2* is the ultimate in ships, personnel and passengers! The captain was Captain Woodall. I liked having him in charge because I now equated him with his wife who said I was the *QE2* Diva! Also aboard was the cruise staff of Lindsay Frost, Les Rolinson, Larry Szabo and Elaine Mackay.

The gangways were raised at 2.30 p.m. I always arrived at the New York pier at about twelve noon. I would sit and wait while eating a snack that I had brought from home to tied me over, from the early morning limousine ride. Then once on board I went to my cabin to check it out and watch for my baggage to arrive. Now, I have been traveling with one large suitcase on wheels, and two extra *QE2* bags and a tote bag to carry on myself with incidentals in it. Over my shoulder I had a small flight bag for my camera, camcorder, recorder and battery charger. That bag over my shoulder was heavy but it was safe with me. Then I had a purse with my passport and ticket. What a change this was from my first trips when I carried just one rather small bag!

It was destined to be another one of my very happy vacations. I had come prepared with all of my gowns plus some new ones. I brought along a new red gown. I'm not used to wearing such a bright color, but for some reason I felt the need for that dress when I bought it. I also bought along a new lace dress. It was white over pink. It had rows of tiered skirt. It was pretty and I knew exactly when I would wear it. Also I had a new white ankle length dress which is a favorite of mine. I do like white very much and this one is perfect for warm summer evenings. With all of this preparation, I knew I would enjoy the voyage.

The first night out, Lindsay Frost introduced the passengers to the cruise staff. After that, there was a presentation of "Radio Daze". The Ted Lorenz Singers and Dancers gave a good performance of nostalgic music. Also there was a bon voyage party with the Mark Joyce Showband and with Christine Trevett and Richard Ried as vocalists. It was a fun night. Of course, I visited the Yacht Club because Keith Ansell was playing the piano there. We know how well I liked his music. Also he would on occasion ask me to sing my perennial favorite, *La Vie en Rose*.

It so happened that this year a group of French people from Seattle, State of Washington, were on their way to Paris, France. They were going to celebrate Bastille Day. It was the 14th of July and they were aboard the ship at that precise time. We were in the Yacht Club when we got to know each other. They also knew that I was familiar with the French language, although in a limited way. They asked me to sing for them. Since I knew very well my special French song they asked me to sing. I said that I would but only if Keith Ansell, the piano player, would agree to it. He did agree and I sang the entire song including the introductory verse. It worked out very well. They stood up around me waving a small French flag. It was a happy group. After the little celebration was over, they gave me the little French flag as a souvenir. I left that evening happily waving it! Yes, *La Vie En Rose*. Life was truly in the pink. I was wearing the red dress that evening, which was a formal evening.

This was destined to be a happy trip. I have just reviewed my album and video and I have a lot to tell you. Even though the schedules were much the same, everything seemed to be developing anew and very nicely. Perhaps I was now getting accustomed to sea travel. I no longer had a feeling of apprehension. I felt myself becoming more relaxed.

The celebrity for this trip was Robert Vaughn. He was the Academy Award and Emmy winning actor. He was aboard to introduce the showing of the film *Superman III* in which he stars. Also, he was interviewed by Lindsay Frost one afternoon. For some reason, probably at a social event, I met him, and he gave me permission to have a picture taken with him. Later, I would also get a picture of him with his daughter. I was pleased!

Now the time when I was to take part in the talent show came around. I was getting more and more adapted to performing. This time I had my pink gown, fan, and basket of real flowers! We find out about that later! However, what was very important was how I would be videoed. Well, the group of French tourists knew of my plight to get a photographer to video the singing. They offered to do the photography. With a bit of review about using the camcorder, they said it would be no problem. I knew they were capable.

The accompanist was always ascertained at the rehearsal. This was usually held at 11 a.m. the day of the show. At the rehearsal, I found that a Madeline Maxwell would be practicing with me. She was unusually adept at sight reading. She was so gifted that she was able to go through three arias with me without having any trouble at all. I was certainly pleased. I knew that whatever it would be necessary for her to accompany me to, she would without hesitation be able to do it. I didn't even need to set a definite schedule of arias for vocalization. I would let her take charge and play whatever suited her. This worked out very well.

It was time to get ready. The show started at 4 p.m. I had already given my camcorder to the Yacht Club friends. Now I was dressed in the pink outfit. However, I needed real flowers in my basket. What to do? What to do? In the rush of the moment, I looked furtively about at the flowers in the Midships Bar. They would be just fine! I asked the bartender if I could use his flowers for my basket. He said I could. They fit in my basket just fine! Now, I was ready!

When I was introduced as Mary Mastony from New Jersey, I went on with confidence. Madeline played a few bars. It would be *Caro Nome*, by Verdi. I very much like this aria because it was a favorite of my brother Michael. It went very well. The next aria that she played a few bars of was *Un Bel Di*, by Puccini. I introduced the aria by dedicating it to Captain Woodall. I said that I thought he would like it because it was a song about the sea. Also, it was his wife who had called me the *QE2* Diva. However, I did not say that on stage. The aria went well. I could count on Madeline to accompany me beautifully. Now two numbers should be enough, but I had such a good accompanist that she was ready for a third. I asked the audience if they would like one more aria. They indicated that they would like one. I told them that I was glad because I had gone to the trouble of stealing the flowers in my basket from the Midshipman's Bar. Of course, everyone laughed, especially the men. They laughed, and laughed and laughed. I told them that they could see a little white napkin where the flowers had been. I then told them that I would return them after the show. It was good fun! I was glad that I was now relaxed enough to be of good humor. Well, I sang the lovely *Si Mi Chiamino Mimi*. I very much like this aria. I could tell from the applause that they liked it also. I looked at the video and it was wonderful. Now I have a record of the three arias. Thank you, Seattle, for taking the video. You were great!

The holidays had really just begun. We would be getting off at Southampton. I had my room changed from #5097 to #2135. This is the time when rooms are changed, for incoming passengers, if necessary. In Southampton I will see the sail boats and know it is the time to take a ride to the New Forest and towns beyond. I like this part of a voyage. I wouldn't mind making a trip to London, but the time is too short to get there and back in time for the ship.

We went to the New Forest and to Lymington. There I took my walk down to the quay. It is such a lovely spot. It is so picturesque. The shops along the way had many varieties of flowers along the front of their stores. I couldn't get enough of the pretty flowers in bloom in the front of the stores. I took a full roll of film of the blossoms. It was a great day. It usually is nice when I'm in Lymington.

Back on board! Captain Robin Woodall was in charge. We would be leaving on the 17th of July and arrive in Bergen, Norway on the 19th. The cruise staff was much the same. It was good to have a stable staff that you could feel comfortable with on recurring trips. We had the usual bon voyage party night. Then, of course, the visit to the Yacht Club to drink Perrier and enjoy the music of Keith Ansell. I would often go in to hear him before dinner at 7.30 p.m. and then again after dinner and after some of the shows! Then I went to the midnight buffet and later spent some time at the piano in the Midships Lobby which was close to my cabin.

We were on passage to Bergen, the home town of the composer Edvard Grieg. As you know, I had seen his house before, but I was glad to see it again. There is something to learn and see every time we visit. I recalled Colin Brown playing my copy of Grieg's *Concerto in A Minor*, so well, at about this time in the trip.

At 8.30 a.m. the *QE2* docked at Bergen. My tour left at 9 a.m. for Bergen and Troldhaugen. We arrived at Troldhaugen, there we saw again the small flat-roofed buildings covered with grass. And, of course, further up the hill we again saw the home of Grieg. I just went in to look at the piano again. However, this time we had an opportunity to walk around the lake. The tour leader then told us an interesting story about the composer that I had not heard on the last trip. Apparently he enjoyed going out on the lake in a small fishing boat. It was relaxing for him. He very much liked the way the sun shined on the lake making it glisten. He also noted that the sun shined on a sheer faced rock formation near the lake. It came to him that it was that place in which he wanted to be buried. So a tomb was carved out of the sheer wall of the rock. There Grieg was eventually buried. There is a plaque there in his memory. Also every year on the date of his death, the townsfolk remember him with special ceremonies.

We were then taken to visit the Church of St Mary's. It was an interesting example of Romanesque architecture. It was a beautiful church with lovely religious paintings. We had not been taken to the Fantoff Stave Church because it had recently been destroyed by fire. As you know I had seen it on my other trip to Norway. I was saddened to know about the fire. However, the stave churches, of which there are very few left, burn quickly because they are made entirely of wood. I hope great care will be taken of those stave churches that are left.

The comfort of the evening dinner aboard ship and the evening of entertainment made the day complete after a tour. As you know, I always enjoyed the Mark Joyce Showband featuring Christine Trevett. And then, of course, a listen in the Yacht Club to Keith Ansell. How could one be so lucky?!

The next day we were in the port of Hammerfest. The launches left early in the morning. We would have a limited time ashore because at 1.30 p.m. we would leave for the North Cape. Hammerfest was a small fishing village started in 1871. The only thing of interest was the shopping area in the city center. I decided to go off to the right of the center. I decided to walk toward a hill from which I hoped I might be able to see the *QE2* from above. As I walked along I heard some lovely classical guitar music. It was a student musician. I went to him. He was playing some songs that I recognized. My father was a violinist but also a good guitarist. He gave lessons in guitar. So I very much enjoyed meeting up with this guitarist whose name was Peter. We talked. He told me he had done some studying in London. Also, he said that he had some cassettes for sale. I was glad to buy a cassette from him titled "Pete Plays Classical Guitar". He was glad to have a buyer. Then with the sound of the guitar music in my ears, I continued walking up the long hill. Along the way, there were so many beautiful flower boxes and small gardens along the street. I again became engrossed in their beauty. I took pictures of as many different varieties as I could find. Then I continued walking until I reached the top of the hill. There I stood and looked about. Sure enough, down below I could see the *QE2*. What a beautiful sight! It was worth the walk and the music I found along the way! I will always remember Hammerfest.

Thank you, Peter, for the guitar music! I wish my dad had been there with me to hear you!

We left for the North Cape. There one could take a tour but the drive up mountains didn't appeal to me. I stayed in the small fishing village at the base of the mountains. There, sales people in their Lapland dress sold souvenirs. There were a lot of fur pieces on racks. Those were certainly too big for a traveler to buy or need. I looked about and finally found a white deer fur muff! It was so appealing and putting my hands into it, I thought I might use it on winter days in New Jersey. Whatever, it was the most representative souvenir of the North Cape that I could find. The ship had anchored at 6 p.m. so it was well after that that we were busy making our purchases. I walked about admiring the scenery at that hour. Then I strolled down an open road to purchase some film at an isolated restaurant at the top of a hill. I could see the reindeer grazing. It was now about 10 p.m. It was a different world.

The best part of being at the North Cape was when we all got together on the open deck at midnight to celebrate seeing the sun at that strange hour. I was looking forward to the fun! We did have a good time. The midnight sun was out in great splendor. The MC of the evening, Jim Bowen, kept us all in stitches. He was so funny. There wasn't anything that he didn't think of to make us laugh. I enjoyed it. Then he had us join in a song fest of easy old-time favorites. Of course, I made my usual list of songs. Here are some: *Bye, Bye Blackbird, I'm Forever Blowing Bubbles, We're Little Black Sheep That Lost Our Way*, and *Edelweiss*. We sounded great on the ocean air with the midnight sun shining above!

I saw Christine and Mark Joyce there also having a good time. They deserved an evening under the sun at midnight! We enjoyed all of the good entertainment they had provided during the trip!

The next day we were on passage towards Hellesylt and Geiranger. It was a day to enjoy on-board activities. The schedule was diverse enough to keep everyone occupied and content. The library is often a good choice. However, I chose to hear a lecture on "Fjordland". The lecturer told us about my favorite palace, Geiranger. I was looking forward to being there again.

Some passengers disembarked at Hellesylt to take an overland tour over to Geiranger. They would meet us again there. I wanted to go directly to Geiranger Fjord. It was my "R and R". This day when I arrived there, a passenger from my table was happily eating an ice cream cone. An appealing sign advertising Eskimo Ice Cream was strategically placed where the launches docked. We talked and laughed and ended up shopping. She bought some lovely Christmas decorations. I looked for a small reindeer to put under my Christmas tree. We walked around and lingered by a stream coming from a waterfall. Diana wanted to touch the cool water and ended up by slipping on the grass and almost falling in. Oh, my! Then she remembered that she had forgotten to take the tour that she had reserved. Better luck next time, Diana!

Our next port was Stavanger. A shuttle bus was provided for us if we wanted to go to the shopping mall on the outskirts of town. I was looking forward to going because I had a mission. I wanted to look for music for Keith Ansell. He had said he was looking for the *Lime's Theme*. It was a song from a movie. The difficult part for us was to decide what was the name of the film. This I would find out when I arrived at the mall.

The trip to the Stavanger mall was exciting for me. I took my video with me so that every inch of the Norwegian countryside could be filmed. The roads were wonderful; very open, no congestion and occasional outbursts of roadside flowers. I enjoyed the ride provided for us and I have a great video of it. When we arrived there in front of me was a large spread-out mall. I went in and looked for the music score section of the all-inclusive mall. I told the salesman there that I wanted *Lime's Theme*. He said it would come under the name of the film in which it was played. He then looked under *Thin Man*, then *The Tall Man* and finally he said it was *The Third Man*. Well, that was solved. However, he did not have the music, so I bought another popular song! Then I wandered about and enjoyed the mall.

Walking back to the *QE2*, the Norwegian scene with its small fishing boats is lovely. There were statues to their heroes, usually named Christiansen, also my sister-in-law's name. The fish stands were busy with their customers, as I passed by, preparing to board the ship again. This was our last Norwegian port. I lingered as I looked out at the little houses so close together, the fishing boats and the statue. I reflected a moment and then showed my boarding pass. It had been a nice visit!

The entertainment for the evening consisted of a variety showcase. On the bill were Alan Randall, multi-instrumentalist, the dynamic Christine Trevett, "Zane" the extraordinary magician and illusionist and the great special host whom we all loved, Jim Bowen! Of course, there was the usual dream time to listen to my favorite piano player, Keith Ansell. At one point Keith allowed me to tape his music which I brought home to my dear brother. At the time, he was not feeling well and had been operated upon. I knew how much he missed his music. So, I brought Keith's tape for him to listen to when he was recuperating. He appreciated it but hoped that I had not bothered that kind musician!

This would be the test of my endurance. I knew that Jim Bowen would be the Master of Ceremonies for the talent show.

What to do? What to do? I was really apprehensive about going on the stage because I knew he would say something very funny. That might jar me a bit in presenting my aria. Nevertheless, the show must go on!

I got dressed for the occasion, wearing the pink gown that I had become accustomed to wearing. I had my pink fan and a basket of flowers. I believe I must have thought I would sing three arias as I had done on the trip crossing. I was ready with all of the other trappings, such as camera, recorder and video camcorder. My accompanist was Madeline Maxwell.

Jim Bowen finally came to introduce me. He said "Now we have a bit of opera. You know opera is serious singing? Yes, it is serious singing." It was all right but he is so funny that anything he says is funny! Well, I went on stage stronger than in the past and I said, "It's every opera singer's nightmare to be introduced by a comedian and I happen to have been introduced by the best comedian in all of England!" It was all in good fun!

I sang *Caro Nome*. Then I sang *Si Mi Chiamino Mimi*. All went well. However, would I make it to sing that ship's favorite *Un Bel Di*? I could see that Jim was getting a little nervous about the time element. He wanted to get on with his repartee and another act. Somehow, I gave it a chance. Well, there is a part in the aria in which I sing that I see a little man on the horizon. It would be Butterfly's long gone husband. At this point, Jim came on stage with a cup of coffee. Of course, he got the attention and laughter. I, like the distressed opera singer walked off the stage. It was so much fun! We knew we had pleased the audience. We are great friends. Thank you, Jim, for your good humor and the great book that you wrote!

For the return voyage, the captain was Captain Robin Woodall. The cruise staff would have on board Peter Longley again. He had been away to get married to Bettine Clement. I met her and thought she was a very nice person besides being an excellent flautist. She performed later on during the crossing. The rest of the cruise staff was much the same, making the return pleasant.

The five day crossing was spent as usual. Dining with a new group. We had a doctor and a nurse at our table. I went to the evening show in the Grand Lounge. My favorite was the Mark Joyce Showband featuring Christine Trevett. They always had a sensational performance. And, of course, I made my visit to hear Keith play his great popular music. I failed to mention that on my visit to hear him play after our trip to Stavanger, I told him that I couldn't locate *Lime's Theme*. I also mentioned that we were confused about the name of the film. I mentioned the names we thought of that were not right. He offered another name, *The Fat Man*. I, of course, told him it was *The Third Man*. That evening he played some great songs from the *Phantom of the Opera* and other lovely songs. My list was: *All The Things You Are, This Can't Be Love and You Are The Promise Kiss of Springtime.* I liked them all.

To add to the sociability of the passengers, sometimes we received invitations to small cocktail parties given by the officers. This trip I received two. One was from Dr Andrew Eardley, the principal medical officer of the voyage and Dr Martin Carroll, the assistant medical officer. It was a lovely evening and a nice diversion. It gave us an opportunity to meet people other than those you meet at your table at dinner. That same night I attended another party in the boardroom (on boat deck) given by John Duffy the hotel manager. It also was a good party with many more people to meet. Sometimes you even meet someone from your home town or the vicinity of it. This starts some interesting conversation!

At 10 p.m. that same night there was a concert in the theater. It was called a classical soirée with music by Bach, Mozart and Vivaldi featuring Bettine Clement on flute and

Daniel Heifetz on violin. It was a wonderful concert. I enjoyed the music very much and it was certainly a pleasure to hear Peter Longley's wife, Bettine, perform so well. She was wearing a lovely blue sequined gown and her musical presentation with the violinist was great to see and hear. Thank you, Bettine!

It was the last full day aboard. Captain Robin Woodall invited all Cunard World Club Members for cocktails. It was held in the morning between 11 a.m. and 12.30 p.m. in the Queen's Room. My talent show rehearsal was at 11 a.m., but I was able to attend after the rehearsal. I always liked to attend this party because it was at such a party as this that Mrs Woodall first called me the *QE2* Diva!

For those who had time that morning, Kitty Kelley, award winning author gave a lecture on "What's Wrong with American Journalism". Also Rex Reed was in the theater. He is a critic for the New York Observer. I had often listened to him on the radio. Then in the afternoon, Robert Vaughn was interviewed by Peter Longley, the cruise director.

As usual at about 3 p.m. I prepared for the talent show. It wasn't easy to collect everything together. I wore the pretty lace gown. It was white lace with an under-gown of pink taffeta. With me I had my sheet music, my camera, my recorder and my video! As I walked past the cruise center, Elaine Mackay saw me and said she liked my gown because it was lace. She said that she liked lace.

I sang *Si Mi Chiamino Mimi*. Yes, I carried a basket of flowers! I also sang *Un Bel Di*. Yes, I had my fan! These, of course, added to my preparatory measures! My accompanist was again the fabulously talented Madeline Maxwell. All went well. We received a great deal of applause. Now I have a lovely video to remember the occasion. I don't know who took the video. However, it was very well photographed. Thank you, whoever you may be. Also thank you, Madeline Maxwell! May God bless you and the music you give so beautifully to others!

Home again! This time I would be looking into the construction of a new townhouse called the "Scottish Highlands"! These townhouses were being built of stone and looked to me like Edinburgh Castle! Of course, I, the dreamer, would like this. I put the end unit on hold. If all went well it would be finished by Christmas. I would then be able to take a world cruise on the *QE2* in January. My friends aboard ship seemed to think it was doubtful that it would be ready, even though I had been told by the builders that it would be finished. I'll explain!

Chapter Eleven
Caribbean 1994

It was no secret that I had been looking for a new home. This quest had been intermittently part of my active schedule. I had come very close to making a purchase in the area of my brother's family. New homes were being built there. This was fine because it was also close to Rutgers University which I was attending. It was a lovely home. However, my decision was negative.

Then came another close call that involved a more difficult decision. That was a gorgeous home in Florida. My brother's family had a condominium there next to a lovely lake. I thought it was ideal and that I might find a home there. I found a large spacious house with an indoor pool situated in a spacious foyer. Also, the house was next door to that of Burt Reynolds, the actor. There he had an acting studio. This might be nice. Then I could invite family and relatives to visit during the winter. However, the answer was negative again. It was too big.

I went on making trips to Florida, all by myself, with the aim of a new house in mind. This time I thought I might have found just what I wanted. It was a beautiful pink stucco house with a red-tiled roof. It was the end house of a group of new single homes attached in groups of four. This house was lovely. In its front yard was a constructed waterfall. It looked beautiful and cool! The house was on one level with a garage.

It had been completely furnished by an interior decorator in modern Floridian white furniture. I liked it. It also meant that I didn't need to go out looking for furniture appropriate to the surroundings.

I went one weekend in November that I had free to sign a contract. However, once more the decision was negative. At that time of year most snowbirds had returned north. It was clear that it was not really advisable to spend the whole year in Florida! I was too far away from all of my activities in New Jersey. Whatever, I came back from Florida without buying a home there.

Next I began looking for a home in the New Jersey area. I would be able to transfer my furniture more easily. Also it was closer to where I was involved in activities connected with school, family and friends. It so happened that the "Scottish Highlands", a group of luxury townhouses were being built. The brochure was really inviting. They were to be built of stone to look like a Scottish castle. Oh, they were lovely. After many visits to the site I put a hold on an end unit. It was located exactly where I wanted to live. Now, I just had to wait. In the meantime, I went on the 1993 cruise that I told you about in the last chapter.

Now the moment of truth had come! Daily I went to see the construction work. It was going well. The excitement of seeing the progress from bottom to top and the walls being built was my daily joy. With camera in hand, I believe that I captured every phase of the building stages. I couldn't wait!

With the expectation of the house being built and ready for occupancy before Christmas, I sent in my reservation to take the 1994 World Cruise around the world. I paid for the booking in one. That is, I paid the fare from New York to New York! I was very much looking forward to this particular itinerary. Also, I was looking forward to the opportunity to be on board with all of the wonderful personnel.

The "Scottish Highlands" home would be a dream come true! It was being built of stone, three levels high and situated in the lovely rolling hills of New Jersey. Now I was beside myself with anticipation. I knew from the plans that it was just right for my needs. After all of this deliberation I decided that this definitely was the new home that I had always wanted. Also, it could be called my castle. It was three stories high and it reminded me of the beautiful castles that I had seen in Scotland.

House plans were coinciding with travel plans in close proximity. I had to come to some definite assurance that the house would be completed as scheduled by Christmas. After much daily inquiry, it was finally confirmed that they could not be completed until a later date. That date they were not sure of but it caused me to cancel the around the world voyage. I informed the travel agent. She was kind and helpful and was able to return to me the full price of the trip. Fortunately, I was under the cancellation date. She is a very good travel agent. She has always been helpful with all of my travel plans. Thank you, Dorothy Reminick!

Now with the trip canceled, moving plans were made. It isn't easy to take all of one's possessions and have them prepared for moving. I worked on it every moment of the day until everything was gathered. Finally in March 1994 the townhouses were completed and I was able to have the movers come by at the end of the month. Finally the day came to move. It was very exciting. I was going into a new home – my castle. Many days were spent eating out for breakfast, lunch and dinner, while all of my belongings were in transit. However, it was comforting to know that I had made the move!

Since it was not possible to go on the around the world voyage, I decided to settle for the Caribbean cruise. It would be leaving from New York upon its completion of the circumnavigation. It would be nice to see friends that I missed. Therefore, I made reservations for Wednesday, 13th April, 1994.

We had had a very cold and snowy winter. Now in the spring it seemed a little chilly. I'm used to getting aboard ship in warm weather. However, for this trip I wore a black wool suit. It felt comfortable. I had the usual suitcases filled with the gowns I loved plus two new ones.

I departed from my brother's home. There I said my goodbyes. When I returned I would also go there to welcome them on my homecoming. My brother had not been feeling well. I had lately been going on my trips concerned about him. However, he had the loveliest wife who would do everything for him as he had always done for her. They were a good couple.

I arrived at the pier in New York. It is always a happy feeling being there. I knew I would soon be in good company. I was going to see friends and talk about their trip around the world which I had not been able to take. Upon arriving on board, I went to the Purser's office. The Purser's office is the hub of the ship's activities. It is here that all questions about cabins and restaurant assignments are answered. It is also a place to buy stamps and have your currency changed. In general it is a place to find out what you need to know.

On this occasion I met my travel agent for the first time. We had always corresponded by mail or by phone whenever reservations were made. This time she happened to be aboard the ship for a meeting. She recognized me immediately. She had made my ticket so I guess she knew just where I would be at that time. It was nice to meet her because she was always very helpful in making my travel reservations.

While in the Purser's office Keith Ansell walked in! I was surprised to see him. He was surprised to see me. Of course, I had decided on the vacation at the last minute. I needed a break from the pressure of buying and moving into a new home. Keith had made the trip around the world. He found it to be a bit lonely. I guess he was glad to be getting close to home.

Captain John Burton-Hall was in charge on this trip. The cruise director was Peter Longley, the social director was Andrew Graham and the social directress was Elaine Mackay. I considered all of them to be my friends. It was good to see and travel again with them aboard.

This trip was a chance to relax. I didn't have plans for seeing anything that I hadn't seen before on my other Caribbean cruise in 1992. However, we were going to St Lucia which I had not seen. I was looking forward to being there.

Each day I followed the schedule at hand. It was enjoyable to sunbathe on the deck. It was nice to go to the library and look up material of interest. Also I liked having lunch in the Lido. There I could have a buffet type meal. I could make my own selection and do it quicker. After lunch I went to the laundry room to press my clothes in preparation for the days when I would be too busy to do so. I wrote and sent cards to my friends everywhere. I played the piano to my heart's content. All of the activities kept me happy!

Our first port of call was Port Everglades. I selected the tour to Miami and the Seaquarium. I had never been to Miami. I had heard so much about this resort that I was looking forward to seeing it. We were driven around Miami a bit. Then we had some time on our own to do as we wished. I chose to look at the lovely sandy beaches and then go to the mall where the bus was parked. It was the usual shopping mall with people busily shopping and looking for items of necessity or trivia. I made my phone call to New Jersey from one of the phone booths. Later, I took a shuttle bus to the Galleria Shopping Mall. There I met some people from the *QE2* who were also shopping. It was a pleasant day.

In the evening the entertainer in the theater was Tony Sandler. I had heard him on American television. He and a company of performers sang some good renditions of popular favorites. I, however, preferred going to the Yacht Club to hear Keith Ansell on the piano. There I could really relax and forget all my worldly cares. If there was a song that he didn't have in his repertoire, I would try to find a copy of the song in my music collections that I brought aboard. This evening I looked for *Moonlight Cocktail*.

We were now on passage to St Thomas. The weather on deck was lovely. I met a travel agent from Florida who had been on the around the world voyage. She told me how much she had enjoyed it. We talked about this and that. She gave me a picture of Sydney Harbor. I would like to visit the opera house there some day. She told me that she would like to make travel arrangements for me if I wished. I told her that I had a travel agent. However, I thanked her for her offer.

It so happened that my favorite piano player's schedule was changed. He would be playing for lunchtime cocktails from noon to 1 p.m. by the Midships Bar. It was a lovely place to play the piano because one could look directly out to the ocean. I liked it there and went there before lunch. He also played the piano there from 6 p.m. until 7.30 p.m. Whenever possible I went there before dinner. It was the one bit of quiet home-like atmosphere on the ship. Keith was always kind and gave me a cordial greeting. He knew that I appreciated his piano interpretations. I have a note to find the song *Green Eyes*.

We arrived off Charlotte Amalie, St Thomas. There were many tours. In fact, there were nine: Kon Tiki Carnival, Atlantis Submarine, Helicopter Sights, Buck Island Sail, Magen's Bay, Coral World, Explorer and Seaplane Adventure. I chose none of these. Again, I preferred to shop in the lovely shops there. I liked to look at linen and jewelry. I took a nice sunny walk up to the Windward hotel and watched the small boats in the harbor. It is a picturesque island discovered in 1493 by Columbus. Now it is a tourist attraction.

Monday, the 18th, we were anchored off St Lucia. I remember seeing the lovely green volcanic-type island. It looked rather small in comparison to the other islands. The ship anchored off Castries, St Lucia. There we took a launch to the island. The weather was a bit overcast. I didn't have anything of interest to do except to peruse the stores. Since I had not bought an emerald ring, which I had thought would be special to buy in the Caribbean, I decided to spend the day looking for one. I had looked for one on the other islands, but they were always too expensive. Now that I had the time, I thought I would take another approach. I would ask for the 'least expensive' emerald ring that they had in the jewelry shop. With that request, the sales clerk showed me two rings that were just short of one hundred dollars. Since others that I had seen were more like four thousand dollars, I thought this to be a bargain. Remember, however, the stones were small. They were, nevertheless, emeralds. I decided to buy one of the rings. It was very pretty. A customer next to me said he liked it also. I walked out wearing it with joy! It will always remind me of that misty day in St Lucia!

Back aboard ship I followed the usual routine. It was always pleasing to me. Now, I was wearing my little emerald ring and that added to the pleasure!

Our next port of call was Barbados. It is the most easterly of the Caribbean Islands. It is very English. I believe it is the home of the ship's doctor, Nigel Roberts. The center of the town has a place called Trafalgar Square. Bridgetown is the capital city. They have towns, such as Yorkshire, reminiscent of England. Also, they drive on the left side of the road.

After a great day of walking around Barbados enjoying the sights and shopping, I bought a Caribbean-blue bow-tie and cummerbund for the piano player in the Yacht Club. He was always kind and respectful. At 3.30 p.m., the Barbados steel band played music typical of the island. Then at 4.45 p.m., on one deck, there was a sailaway party. Gentlemen were asked to wear their brightest shirts and ladies to wear their most colorful dresses. There on deck gentlemen hosts and passengers were invited to dance. Complimentary punch was served. It was all in good fun as we left the island of Barbados.

In the evening I gave gifts that I had bought for friends among the crew who were so kind in their service. I always seemed to have a wonderful waiter and waitress to whom I enjoyed giving a present along with the gratuity at the end of trips. They were appreciative of my thinking of them. Thank you!

Later on in the evening I had been invited to Dr Andrew Eardley's cocktail party. I was glad to get the invitation because I could wear a new colorful gown. It was a bright multicolored gown of wide stripes of black, rose, white, blue and green. It had a black bow with rhinestone clip at the waist. It was very Caribbean. It was very pretty and perfect for a Caribbean party. I was glad to have the dress and the invitation. Yes, we had a lovely evening meeting new friends. Thank you Dr Eardley and staff!

At dinner, for this trip, I was seated at a table of six. Dr Eardley was the host officer. I asked if they would like to have me say the Grace. I well remembered my mother's prayer at special meals and I thought it would be appropriate at this time. Dr Eardley liked the prayer so much that he asked for a copy. Also, others have liked it and wanted a copy. So here it is:

DINNER GRACE

We thank Thee Lord for this our food,
For life and health and every good.
Let honor to our souls be given,
With the bread of life sent down from Heaven.
In His name we ask it all. Amen.

At 8.15 a.m. the *QE2* anchored off Philipsburg. I liked the little launch rides. When I arrived on the island I knew there were many places to explore. There was a linen shop that not only had table linens, but also blouses and dresses made of linen. They were great for summer and I took the opportunity to buy a cool-looking blouse. I also bought bright earrings at the open-air market. This was all relaxing for me.

In the latter part of the day I prepared for the very special cocktail party. This was an invitation from the Captain and Mrs John Burton-Hall. It was a gold-trimmed invitation. I considered this a great honor. The party was to be held in his quarters. The passengers could be escorted by their steward if they were not sure about where the officers' quarters were. I was pleased. For this event I wore another new gown. It was a very light pink taffeta gown with a very light pink rose at the waist. It had tiny shoulder straps. I thought it was very poetic.

I liked meeting the captain and his wife. His wife knew about me being called the *QE2* Diva and she addressed me the same way. We were familiar with each other from previous trips. It was a wonderful party. It is always a pleasure to have such a nice gathering of friends before dinner. There, also, was Elaine Mackay who always greeted the guests so warmly. It was a success. Thank you, Captain and Mrs John Burton-Hall.

That evening the chefs were setting up wonderful, sumptuous and beautifully presented delicacies and incredible ice carvings. It was a gala midnight buffet when they did this! Everyone enjoyed the food and artistic endeavors. Thank you!

It was now time for the talent show rehearsal. I made my appearance at the cruise office to sign up. Then I went to the stage, starboard side, to wait for my turn to rehearse. This time around I had an accompanist that I had not had before. It is more time-consuming to show the music intended and to practice arias that are not easy to accompany. However, I was thankful for his good work at such short notice. We did very well. Thank you Stewart Wallaks.

That afternoon I went to the talent show. I wore what had become my favorite singing gown. It was the pink gown with matching pink sequined bodice. I chose two arias that were easier to accompany than others I had sung on previous trips. The Master of Ceremonies was a very special social director from Australia. He was Andrew Graham. He gave me a lovely introduction. When I came on stage, I thanked the staff for their good work in making the trip so pleasant. Also I thanked the waiters and personnel who were very kind. I thought it was a good time for the passengers to show that we appreciated the *QE2* and all it had done for us. I had brought my recorder on stage. I told everyone that I brought it on stage because I liked to hear them clap. That they did!

After being nicely introduced by Andrew Graham I sang the aria *O Mio Babbino Caro* by Puccini. It is such a lovely aria everyone enjoyed it and clapped loudly. It was obvious that they wanted me to sing another. I then sang the beautiful *Caro Nome* by Verdi. It went well. I have the recorded tape and just listened to it. The audience really clapped. Then Andrew asked if I had another to sing. However, I had only planned for two arias at the rehearsal. It was nice to be asked. Thank you one and all! Thank you Andrew Graham!

The evening following the talent show, it was a good feeling to just enjoy the evening. Many times passengers would come to me and tell me that they had heard me sing and congratulated me. It was music to my ears! Sometimes passengers said that they had made a video of the show. That also was a complimentary feeling.

Our next port of call was Fort Lauderdale. There I called my brother's family to tell them I would soon be seeing them. Then I took a shuttle bus to the Galleria Mall. It was the last opportunity to shop. I always found some small memento.

It was time for the goodbyes. The waiters and waitress at my table had been so good it was difficult to leave them. I bought a hair bow for Sarah. I was always as generous as possible with the gratuity at the end of my trips. The service was really exceptional. Thank you Sarah and Paul! Yes, I remember you!

I'm reminded of a bit of humor concerning gratuity envelopes. It was the custom to find a pile of gratuity envelopes in the Purser's office a day or two before the end of a cruise. It so happens that for some reason I have trouble with some of my high-heeled slippers. They seen to want to fall off my feet! I guess I buy them too big. Whatever the reason, I find myself shuffling along in an over-sized pair. One day I reached into the pile of gratuity envelopes and made myself some impromptu innersoles with the envelopes. On I traveled! I happened to meet the special piano player and told him my problem. I told him my slippers had a tendency to fall off. I told him that I had stuffed gratuity envelopes into my shoes to keep them from falling off my feet. I said that I was still having trouble walking properly. Then with his dry English humor he said, "Maybe you need to put more money into the envelopes"!

The Caribbean holiday was now at a close. In the Grand Lounge at showtime they presented a farewell variety show. It was a comedy type of show that would send us off in a happy mood. For me it had been a wonderful and pleasant break from what lay ahead for me back home. In the limousine to New Jersey I had time to contemplate.

The limousine took me to my brother's home. There I inquired about his health. I found out that his problem was not really getting any better. There would be a road ahead of more and more medical procedures. I wasn't pleased but I continued to have hope. It was now about the 1st of May, 1994. I began visiting as often as I could and helping as much as possible. His wife was so very helpful and patient. The two of us would always be alert to his needs. However, at this point he was functioning as normal. He needed attention for doctor's visits and occasional minor surgery. I was home to help and I was glad of that.

Upon arriving at my home, I had much to do. I had left some of the furniture at my former house. It was the bedroom furniture and I needed that to spend my first night in the 'castle'! That first night was scary, but I had friends who phoned me to talk and make it easier. After that first night, believe me, I was one busy person.

My plan was to start with the window treatments. The house had twenty windows to take into consideration. Many were tall Palladian windows. They are impressive to look at but difficult to handle. Special orders had to be made.

Next in order was to hang my many oil paintings in their proper places. I have a collection of twenty-six. They are special because I painted them myself, during my painting phase, as I like to call it. The task was to select the proper place to display them and the physical feat of actually suspending them on the new walls. I did this by myself. I was constantly at the hardware store buying the proper kinds of nails to do the work. Also I had to buy a ladder to get to the high places. However, I loved the paintings and nothing would deter me from giving them a good home in the proper light that they deserved.

Next in order was proper lighting in the house itself. Of course all lights were in and covered properly with their appropriate glass shades. However, I wanted a beautiful chandelier for the dining room. I also wanted a spotlight for a painting over the fireplace. I have a gas fireplace, which I prefer to the wood-burning type. To continue, I found the chandelier after quite a bit of searching. It is entirely of crystal with no brass exposed. Then I had to find an electrician to install the fixtures. It was worth the trouble. The chandelier is simply gorgeous.

The most important item that I wanted for the new home was a piano. I had been playing on a Baldwin low console type. I wanted a white baby grand. However, I had been too busy to go out looking for the exact make and tone that would please me. I had to put that wish on hold!

It was now summer. My brother's family had a house at the shore. It was at Spring Lake, New Jersey. It is a beautiful shore city dominated by a church built on the order of St Peter's Basilica in Rome. It is set near the ocean and also on a lake. It is so idyllic it seems unreal. There are swans on the lake and little bridges here and there to cross and enjoy the scenery. If you have not been there, do go some summer day! Also, on the outskirts of town is a fabulous restaurant called "Doolans". You might want to try it as well!

After the brief break at Spring Lake, I was back to the new townhouse. I have a lovely deck. I like this very much. However, I needed to buy some urns and flowers to make it suit my taste. Therefore I was in and out of nurseries getting flowers. I also wanted a statue of an angel. After a good deal of looking, I finally found the angel of my choice. It is about eighteen inches tall and about ten inches wide. However, the angel was not placed outdoors. It was placed right in my foyer entrance. There was a reason for this final embellishment to my 'castle'. Seeing it would remind me of my earliest childhood. My mother had dressed me as an angel, I was perhaps not quite two. I had no idea what the wings she had put on me were or why she had so lovingly placed them there. I know that she and my dad took me to church to see a play. When we got there and just as the play started, my father carried me to the stage and placed me on the edge of the stage seated with my legs down and my hands clasped. I sat there very quietly. I had no feeling of apprehension. I knew that I was safe because I could see my parents in the audience. I sat there throughout the play which was the "The Story of the Nativity". I don't know how I could have been so completely at ease. I credit this experience with the reason that I really enjoy being on a stage singing! Now when I see that statue when I enter it brings back a very fond memory!

The year was now winding down. It was now December. I was born in this month as was my brother. He was older by a number of years. He was always watchful of his baby sister. My mother had wanted it that way. We were a happy family! Now Christmas was the big event!

This Christmas was a memorable one! It was the first year in the new townhouse. I would be able to decorate it to my heart's content. I decorated the small tree outside my door with lights. I put a small tree on the kitchen table. I had a large tree in the living room. I had a medium size tree in the entry foyer. I put a small tree in the upper bedroom front window. Then I put electric candles in each window. Of course I had a wreath on the door and garlands of pine going up the entry steps held by red ribbons. It was lovely and festive. After all this was my first Christmas in my new castle!

My concern all the while was for my brother. Christmas would be celebrated in his home. I wanted to be generous with gifts and money. There were special presents that I won't forget. I had seen those watches that light up in the dark. I thought my brother would like that for a gift. I bought one for him and also for friends. Also I bought a lovely train set. I didn't indicate who this present was for, because, in reality I just wanted to please my brother. I knew that we had not had a train around our tree when we were children. I thought it would be fun to have one this Christmas. I wanted so very much to make him happy. He wasn't a well man and I was concerned. We had a wonderful Christmas that year of 1994. I will long remember it!

Jim Bowen hosted the Talent Show. He was great. I have it on video.

A happy moment with Keith Ansell, piano player in the Yacht Club. He accompanied me to *La Vie En Rose*.

Singing *Si Mi Chiamino Mimi*, the new aria for Mother's Day.

Return trip: A formal picture with Keith Ansell – 1994. The piano is outside of the dining room.

Picture taken after singing with accompanist-extraordinaire Naki Ataman.

Representation of an earlier Cunard Ocean Liner displayed in 1995. Thank you, Cunard Line, for your years of sailing pleasure!

Holding a gift of flowers. Thank you all very much.

Singing *O Mio Babbino Caro, Caro Nome* and *Un Bel Di* – 1995. Wearing white opera length gloves.

Chapter Twelve
Scotland Tall Ships and North Cape and Fjords 1995

It's a new year! We wonder what the year ahead has in store for us. It is never clear what lies ahead. People in general seem to console themselves at this time by making New Year's Resolutions. The idea is to make oneself better than the previous year. I guess that by doing this it is hoped that the year will also be a better one or at least as good as the last year!

I started the year with the ever-present hope that my brother would somehow get better. To some extent it was working in that direction. The nurse came three times a week to visit. He was not going to the hospital. His condition was stabilized. On some occasions he did revisit the hospital for tests. However, there were no more big operations. I had become used to driving to his home to spend some time with him and his wife and the friendly nurse that might be there.

Now in my new home, I decided that my parents, whom I had lost before I began my solo trips on the *QE2*, should be interred nearer to my new townhouse. I had heard that a new Chapel Mausoleum had been built. I had received a brochure on the subject late the previous year. I kept it for the time when I could inquire about it. In the month of February I began to find out the particulars for moving them to the beautiful mausoleum. The price was exorbitant. However, weren't they the most wonderful parents a person could have? Yes, they were! I would give my best for them. I made several trips to see the building. It was a beautiful newly constructed stone building with two beautiful stained-glass windows on either side of the entry doors between the tall supporting columns.

As you enter the mauve-carpeted chapel, you see before you at the extreme end an immense stained-glass window that extends from floor to ceiling. It is really impressive. It depicts the risen Christ. The inscription is "Whosoever believeth in me shall never die". In front of this is an altar. Then there are mauve chairs in rows for special days of worship. The ceiling is lit with six chandeliers. And last but not least, appropriate music is piped in softly throughout the building!

I had some decisions to make. I wondered about placement. The walls were all of authentic marble. There were about four beautiful corridors. Where would be the best place to put my beloved parents? I showed the plan to my brother and family. I let them know what I was planning to do. They decided to come with me to look at what I had in mind. They did come and they looked. I asked my brother where he thought the place should be. His answer was that it should be in the chapel part near the door. He thought that at that point there was a lot of light from the outside showing through. With that in mind I made my decision.

During the months of February and early March, all of the necessary plans were made for the transition on the interments. The bill for this was duly paid. The new crypts were selected and they were also paid for. All basic formalities had been completed. Now it was time to set the date and procedure. I decided that I wanted my mother and father to be driven by the front of my new townhouse. They had always shown concern for my welfare. I wanted them to know where I was located.

They would have liked that. I also decided that it should be Easter week.

It was a beautiful Wednesday before Easter. I waited at my new townhouse. The large carrier truck, new and of blue color drove up to my house. It was to me an unbelievable sight. I then drove behind the carrier to the mausoleum. There, after waiting for special encasements, I stood at attention to see my father and then my mother's crypt enter the beautiful chapel. For me it was the most memorable moment of my life! I saw them "lifted up" to the open space for them to be placed side by side. I kneeled and bowed my head in reverence. I will never forget the moment!

The days passed after Easter. Michael was still getting home attention. I was visiting very often. By the end of April I had become used to the thought that he was not making progress toward recuperation. One day, a Wednesday, the 3rd of May, I visited. He looked good. The nurse had just tended to him. Then suddenly he felt sick. We called for the ambulance. We followed to the hospital. He had passed away. The sadness is too much for me to write about but I feel you are my friends and that you understand. His family and I saw him placed next to our parents. It wasn't planned to happen that way but it certainly pleased me to see that he went in dignity. His wife has a place for herself next to him when that day should come. God bless my brother Michael forever.

The sadness I felt and still feel I can't describe. I spent my days thereafter visiting the mausoleum. My heart was so full of sorrow that I didn't find interest in anything including the new townhouse. Finally I realized this could not go on. I must do something to relieve my aching heart. So, my thought was that perhaps I should make a reservation for the summer trip to the North Cape. However, I did not want to go. I had lost my interest in singing. I kept refusing to make a reservation.

Finally, I thought I should make myself do it regardless of whether I wanted to or not. With courage, I called my travel agent and made the reservation for the North Cape cruise.

I immersed myself in preparations for the trip. Packing my bags would not let me forget but it kept me busy. I had all of the necessities. I didn't need to buy a new gown. I had enough. I didn't do any singing. I knew my arias so well. I didn't feel like singing, but I brought my music in the hope that I would feel better. It wasn't long before I had everything in readiness to leave. Now I would be leaving my castle. It was a difficult feeling. However, I knew it was best to leave and see my *QE2* friends.

My brother's family and friends were very supportive of my taking the trip. Also, my teacher friend Larry was supportive, although he didn't like to see me go. For this cruise he bought me a beautiful doll to take as my companion. It was thoughtful of him. Yes, the doll was a good companion. Thank you, Larry!

On Monday the 10th of July, 1995, I got into the limousine with doll and baggage, destination the New York pier. Arriving in New York, there was the regal looking *QE2*. The sight of it brightened my outlook. Yes, I had made the right decision!

On board was Captain John Burton-Hall. That was nice to know. It is like visiting in the home of a friend when you have a captain whom you have sailed with before. Also the great Mark Joyce Showband was aboard. This was good to know because I liked his music. The principal medical officer was Nigel Roberts. Of course I knew him because I had sat at his table on other trips. He and I were travel friends. Also the medical officer was Martin Carroll. I had also met him on other trips. The social director was Andrew Graham. He was the Australian who was MC on my last trip. He was a pleasant person. The social directress on board was Maureen Ryan. It was a great family of friends. It might help me forget my cares. I hoped!

First things first. I went to my room 4046. There I found two flower arrangements at my door. One was from the travel agent and the other was from a friend. I liked my room. They have always been small but cozy. I didn't mind what level I had. The first thing I did was to walk around the deck. It was a lovely day and it felt good to be on board. I was feeling better. On deck Doctor Nigel was talking to someone. When he finished I went over and spoke to him. It was pleasant for both of us to see each other again. I guess that is what life is all about, greeting our friends and acquaintances. The sailaway music on deck made it even more congenial.

Later that afternoon we had the usual boat drill. It was even reassuring to put on my orange-colored jacket and find my way to the designated station. Yes, I was feeling at peace on this reluctant "holiday" as the British say!

The ship had been recently refitted to meet the needs of the 21st century. I would be seeing it for the first time. Would I like the changes? The first change I noticed was in the Yacht Club.

It had been completely refitted. The wonderful white Lucite Shimmel grand piano was gone! The carpeting that had made it such a quiet restful spot was gone. It was changed so much that it was no longer recognizable as the familiar Yacht Club that I knew and liked. I turned to leave, when in the small exit portion, in a corner, I saw a display case with the beautiful silver loving cup that had graced the entrance of the Columbia restaurant. I was beginning not to like the changes. Was I the only one who didn't like the changes? I would be finding out later. I had not as yet seen the other changes.

My dining table was now in the Coronia restaurant. It was where the Mauritania restaurant had been located. I didn't like the change. I missed the silver loving cup. Here instead was a huge sculpture of horses placed in circular formation. It was a striking center piece for the restaurant but I would need to get used to it.

My table companions were truly great. We had a pilot and a stewardess who were on their honeymoon. They were very good company. Our table was hosted by the Chief Officer, John Scott. Among the others were a doctor and his wife from Scotland. Also another couple from Scotland. They were all friendly and good company. I was soon forgetting my sorrow and enjoying being on the *QE2* again.

The second day aboard, I walked about finding out about the other changes that had been made. I found out that the wonderful double staircase leading to the shopping level from the stage had been taken away. This made me feel sorry. I liked those stairs! Then, as I continued to look about the ship, I found another big change. The Lido, which had been another escape for me, was gone. The lovely tree decor was gone. The pool that had been there was gone. The carpeted floor, which was a safety measure, was gone. The beautiful super dome was gone. In its place was a very modern cafeteria. I guess the changes were made in preparation for increased travel in the future. However, I must admit that I missed my traditional ship of a year ago!

The first full day out to sea we were invited to the captain's cocktail party. It would be held before dinner in the Queen's Room. The Queen's Room had not been changed much. However, the soft leather upholstered lounge chairs were gone. In their place were new chairs that I didn't like as much. However, I did like the passengers as much as ever. Since it was a formal evening, I wore a pink dress that was very pretty.

It was long in the back and shorter in the front. It was a different look but very nice. In my hair I wore a pink flower from the floral arrangements that I had received. I wanted to feel happy and ready for the party. I brought my camera. I like to take photos of the events. I was able to get a good picture of the captain and myself for my album.

After dinner there was a classical concert in the theater. The pianist Daphne Spottiswoode would be performing the works of Beethoven and Chopin. I do enjoy the music of these two composers, so I went to the theater to hear her. As I walked into the theater to find my seat, at the rear of the auditorium, I saw a gentleman. I was a bit surprised. He had a mustache. He looked like Detective Poirot on television in the "Mystery" series. I just could not help saying to him, "You look like a detective". He then replied by saying that he was a detective. I counteracted by saying that he wasn't. This continued until finally he admitted that he was a concert pianist. Well! Well! Well! I had always looked for a concert pianist to accompany me in the talent show. However, I was usually given a popular piano player. Although some were good, I preferred the classical sight reading accompanist. When he said that he was a concert pianist, I immediately asked him if he would accompany me in the up-coming talent show. He said he would if he could get permission. Now, I was again glad that I had made the decision to take this trip.

The next day I looked over the daily schedule. I found that the entertainment for the evening was the music of the concert pianist 'detective'. He would be performing at 9 p.m. and also at 10 p.m. The theme of his concert was around the world. He was billed as the Turkish cultural ambassador. His name was Naki Ataman and he would present a musical tribute to twenty-five countries. I was looking forward to the evening.

That day I spent my time listening to the travel manager talk about Southampton and beyond. Later I found a quiet room to take the place of the Yacht Club. It was called the Chart Room. Here there was a piano from the ship Queen Mary. Personally I preferred the white Shimmel piano that had graced the Yacht Club, but this was the alternative. At the piano was David Moore. He had his own style of playing the popular songs. He had accompanied me in a talent show on one occasion. It was relaxing to hear his music. I began making a visit to the Chart Room "between classes'. That was what I called it when I went from one of the ship's scheduled activities to another. We thought it was a good joke!

At 9 p.m. I was there in the Grand Lounge to hear Naki Ataman, the detective turned pianist. At the door we received a program. It had a picture of Mr Ataman and a brief résumé. It stated that he was a native of Ankara, Turkey. He was a concert pianist, composer and arranger. He had been selected to be Turkey's goodwill ambassador. He conceived the idea of a program of piano music representative of countries around the world. With that in mind, the program was composed of songs from twenty-five countries. The best part was yet to come for on the stage there was not only a grand piano but also a giant picture screen.

Mr Ataman came on stage, sat down at the piano and started to play. His first number was *Around the World*. A flag of Spain was flashed on to the screen. He then began playing songs representative of Spain. He followed this by repeating the theme song and then proceeded to play songs representative of another country and its flag was displayed. His arrangements plus the background supportive rhythm from his accompanying bass and drums was most effective. I was really pleased to hear him. As he played I kept thinking of my brother who had very much the same style of arrangements to his popular classics as Mr Ataman had. I was surprised! Had I taken this trip not knowing about this? I was glad I had come! At 9 a.m. every morning a Catholic Holy mass was held in the theater. I attended this Mass. I was able to get to know the Father and ask him to have a special Mass for my brother. He very kindly obliged. Being aboard the *QE2* gave me this special opportunity. I appreciated it!

At 9.30 I began attending the computer class. It was most interesting. I am a good typist. I am typing this book for you as I think about you, the reader. It might be that I should use a computer at some point. It was a good opportunity offered to the passengers. I couldn't attend all of the classes, but I attended as many as I could.

Coming soon was the talent show. Would I have Mr Ataman as my accompanist? I found out when I signed up to participate. He would meet me in the morning to practice the aria I selected. We met and we practiced together. It went well. I gave him the music. The arias were the *O Mio Babbino Caro* by Puccini and *Caro Nome* by Verdi.

For this show I wore the white tiered satin gown and the rhinestone tiara. It is a comfortable gown and I really feel like singing when I wear it. We met at the Grand Lounge stage. I was second on the program. When my turn came I was ready with my recorder. Mr Ataman had been very patient as he waited for my turn. He also waited as I explained each aria. He played and I was thankful to have had him accompany me. He was kind to do it. Thank you Naki. I appreciated it!

We arrived in Southampton on the 15th of July 1995. I had made plans for a tour of the New Forest and cities in that immediate area. The tour was no longer complimentary. It was a beautiful day. We drove though Southampton and viewed the arched walls. Then we continued on to Beaulieu where I reminisced about my family's meeting there at the

Montagu Arms hotel. I wanted to get off but the bus did not stop. I also wanted so badly to get a box of chocolates at the chocolate factory there. However, it wasn't possible.

We drove on to the New Forest and enjoyed the scenery of the thatched-roof dwellings, and the beautiful gardens. This was so English. It was just as I recalled it from my childhood story books. I loved it here.

We then went to the Montagu Mansion. It was such a lovely day. A garden party was being held. The sales ladies were dressed in costumes of the Queen of Hearts. This reminded me of a Halloween church party when I was a child. My mother dressed me as a little Queen of Hearts. There was a souvenir center there. I decided to look for some chocolates. I found a couple of boxes which I bought to give to friends back home. I also found out that the chocolate factory in Beaulieu had closed!

Back aboard the ship, this is the portion of the cruise when the English holiday seekers came on board. I liked that because I might see some of my friends again. There is a period of adjustment for these new passengers to get located and have their practice fire drill. Then everything settles down to enjoying the cruise with the new passengers.

This time we were on passage to Scotland. At 6 p.m. there was a Catholic Holy Mass with Father Gould. This was held in the theater. I again went in respect and remembrance of my brother. There I met the Father. I asked him to say a Mass for my brother as Father Agger before him had done. He asked for my brother's name and said he would have a special Mass for him at the next service.

A nice part about this trip was going to Scotland. It was also great that at my table for this portion of the cruise, I was seated with some Scottish couples. They are always such good company. The officer was the radio engineer; he dined with us a few times. We really had a good time together at mealtimes.

Good company is a big part of a cruise! Thank you people for your greeting cards!

Also aboard from England came England's finest comedian, Jim Bowen and his Red Hot Rhythm Band. They entertained in the new Golden Lion Pub. This was an addition since the ship had been refurbished. Here all kinds of variety entertainment was held. Here passengers could drink and enjoy entertainment. Here they had something new to me called the karaoke. Apparently passengers do impromptu acts for the other passengers. It was a popular place.

It was now time to take a tour to Edinburgh. I was looking forward to seeing that Scottish city again. I wanted to walk down Princes Street again. I wanted to find out if it still gave me an out of body experience. The day of the tour, Princess Anne was to have lunch in the Coronia restaurant. That meant my restaurant would be vacated for her and her entourage. It didn't matter because I would be on a tour of Edinburgh.

The 17th of July, 1995 was a big day aboard ship. We would anchor off Edinburgh, Scotland. There, from Leith, would emanate the Cutty Sark tall ships. The race would honor Leith's nautical heritage on a grand scale. We were all looking forward to the event. Leith had its seafaring traditions dating back nine hundred years. The first steamship to cross the Atlantic Ocean was built there in 1837. Also in 1561, Mary Queen of Scots disembarked at Leith on her return from exile in France. It was an exciting place to see from the deck of the *QE2*.

I chose to take a launch and tour to see the city of Edinburgh. It would bring back memories of my first visit there. At that time I felt as though I was walking on air. The ride by bus was interesting. I loved seeing the Scottish countryside. We finally arrived. I took my long awaited walk and photographed the castles. It was a beautiful day and there was so much to see. I stopped at a bank to change some money to Scotch currency. Then I bought some post cards to send to family and friends. It was great to be there, but I did not walk on air this time!

When we arrived back on the ship, it was time to look at the beautiful sailing ships in the Firth of Forth. It was a very impressive sight to see the tall ships, getting ready for tomorrow's race. That evening the band of Her Majesty's Royal Marines of Scotland gave two performances in the Grand Lounge. The music was unforgettable. I have always liked band music. It was my dad's favorite music also. Then to top off the day's activities, the late night entertainment was a spectacular fireworks display. This was at 10 p.m. on the upper deck aft. It was really exciting. I certainly was glad I had made the trip.

At 9 a.m. I went to the Catholic Holy Mass to hear the special Mass that Father Gould had prepared for my brother Michael. The Mass aboard ship is very reverential and tastefully presented. Father Gould's presentation was so beautiful, with such a descriptive prelude, that I was truly immersed in his every word. When he was finished, I thought there was never such a befitting Mass said anywhere to have compared with this Mass. There again, was this the call to take this trip that I was almost denying myself? I thank you, Father Gould!

From noon to 4.30 p.m., the tall ships parade of sails in the Firth of Forth, took place. There was a commentary on deck by the chairman of the Forth Yacht Club Association. It was a rather misty day but lovely. The ships were racing with crews from different nations taking part. They would race on through the North Sea to Germany, Denmark, the Netherlands and finally reach Belgium. We all enjoyed this special opportunity to see the beginning of this prestigious race. Kudos to the Cunard Line!

In the evening we had an invitation to Captain John Burton-Hall's cocktail party. It was a chance for me to wear the lovely black gown with a skirt of three tiers. It was comfortable and festive with a diamond shaped motif on the front bodice. The evening was pleasant. I drank my orange juice cocktail. I met some new friends. I took some pictures of the officers for the cruise that were introduced by the captain. Everyone seemed to be enjoying the occasion.

After dinner, the entertainment was again showtime with the music of Naki Ataman. He would perform again his "Around the World" concert. Since he reminded me of my brother at the piano and the selections of songs, etc., I went to see both of his performances! I had first taken an ocean voyage in 1985 because of the number of pianos aboard. Now I would hear the ultimate in the music I loved played by an expert in the field. I went to both performances. I would have gone to a third! Mr Ataman was accompanied by Wyn Davis on bass and Mark Joyce on drums. That was great percussion work! Thank you all. Thank you again Mr Ataman. Your music does make you a great cultural ambassador!

Jim Bowen, the English comedian had been on board from Southampton. It was good to see him again. The English passengers really enjoyed his humor. His rhythm band was a good supportive background for his jokes. That day he was signing copies of his book *From a Bundle of Rags*. I was first to go to the library to buy a copy of his book. Jim was very nice to me. He remembered me as the opera singer whom he had introduced on one of our trips. He signed the book and wrote in it, "Best wishes Mary. I enjoyed the opera. *QE2* Norway July 1995. Enjoy the read." Signed Jim Bowen. I did enjoy the read, Jim and I hope we meet again on stage. You are the best! Thank you very much Jim!

That evening I was to hear, for the first time, an Irish-English comic called Tom O'Connor. His humor was quiet and relaxing. Apparently he was born in Ireland but later went to Liverpool, England. I found his type of comedy, that was interspersed with songs typical of England, to be enjoyable. The next day he was signing copies of his book called *Take a Funny Turn*. I bought his book also, which he signed. He also had a cassette with his style of comedy and songs, which I bought. Thank you, Tom!

We arrived at anchor off Skarsvaag in the Ris Fjord. At 6 p.m., from the gangway on five deck aft we went to the tenders which transported us to the shore. There I took my usual walk. I found it very exciting to be walking around this strange northern hemisphere at such a late hour in the evening and yet in the daylight. It was then about 10 p.m. I took some pictures. I spoke to some of the residents. I asked how they lived during the winter months. They said it wasn't bad. They showed me the snow ploughs that they used to clear the roads so they could go for their groceries. I wasn't convinced it would be that easy in the Arctic Circle. I then returned by launch back to the ship.

The main activity for this evening aboard ship was seeing the midnight sun. For this event entertainment was planned. On the last trip you remember we had a wonderful party hosted by Jim Bowen and his Red Hot Rhythm Band. He was funny and we sang some happy singalongs. This year in the Pavilion and Lido there was an Arctic Circle cookout. Being served were hamburgers, hot-dogs, relishes and windjammer soup. It was held indoors and was a bit more formal than the last party. However, the music, Jim Bowen, and the food made for a very happy occasion. I truly enjoyed this trip to the Cape and of course, seeing the sun at midnight!

We were now on our way to Trondheim. A shuttle bus service was provided for us when we arrived. I took the early 9.15 a.m. bus. I could enjoy as much of the day as possible looking around. It so happened that in Trondheim there was an adorable rubber-tired train that ran through the town. On board was a tour driver who explained the sights. It was an open train and a lovely day to enjoy the ride and the carousel music. It may seem childish but many adults were anxious to take the ride. Actually it was for adults as well as children. This gave the city of Trondheim a festive appeal. Later I did some shopping and went back to the ship happily!

The entertainment for the evening was the music of the Turkish Ambassador, Naki Ataman. This evening he had a different theme for his performance. This time the theme was "Try to Remember". It was an evening of the romantic and nostalgic, the classical popular songs as I like to call them. His program consisted of thirty-four songs. All of these were played in one sitting! It took an hour and fifteen minutes. To give you some idea of the songs that he played, here is a list of the first six: *Try to Remember, Days of Wine and Roses, Red Roses for a Blue Lady, La Vie En Rose, Poor Boy of Paris*, and *Secret Love*. He had great command of the piano. He played them all without any music. He was able to hold the interest of the audience through his excellent expression of musical tone, rhythm and shadings of fortissimo and pianissimo. As he played I thought even more that he looked like my brother. He was now playing the songs my brother had often played with his band and by himself.

One evening I was able to tell Mr Ataman how much he reminded me of my brother. I told him that there was one difference. That difference was the mustache that he had, that my brother did not have. He then proceeded to pretend to peel off his mustache. So, I found out, he had a sense of humor as well as being a great piano player.

I bought his two CDs. I am pleased to have them. This was another good reason to be thankful that I had the unknown courage to take this trip. Thank you again, Naki!

Finally we arrived at my very favorite spot, Geiranger. This fjord is so beautiful that I feel at this point I forget all of my cares. I simply enjoy the launch ride and the walk by the ice-cream stand. Everyone looks in a vacation mood. I also like the cozy little picnic tables overlooking the fjord. The waterfalls and the Norwegian houses add to the beauty of the fjord. Thank you *QE2* for including and taking us here on this cruise. I saw my friend Diana again this year. She was walking around. I told her to watch out and not to fall in the stream! Remember last year Diana!

Our last cruise stop was Stavanger. This is an interesting Norwegian town full of life and excitement. At the harbor you linger to look at the quay with its picturesque boats of all sizes. I like to take my usual walk through the bustling center of town to look at the displays in the stores and just enjoy the ambiance of the city. It is a vacation in itself just to be there. I have always been blessed with good weather on my trips, which, of course, were in the height of the summer season.

Back aboard ship, Jim Bowen, with his Hot Rhythm Band was performing in the new Golden Lion Pub not far from the theater bar. In the evening the lovely voice of Christine Trevett could be heard. She had married the band leader, Mark Joyce. They are favorites of mine. I hope they will always be aboard when I am sailing. Congratulations Christine and Mark!

Now the cruise was coming to a close. It was time for the talent show. I knew that I would sing. I enjoy singing for the English passengers before they get off for Southampton. Brian

Price was in charge of the show. He was such a thoughtful person. He said that he would introduce me from the stage. By that I mean, he would allow me to come from behind the stage curtain. This instead of sitting at the side of the stage and walking up some steps to get on stage. This was a big privilege for me. I was definitely pleased. So I prepared and was able to rehearse. I wore the white satin gown with the rhinestone tiara. Also, this time, I wore opera length white gloves. It felt very appropriate for the arias that I would sing. Brian Price was the MC. He didn't have an opening act, so I was listed first on the program. The arias were *O Mio Babbino Caro* by Puccini and *Caro Nome* by Verdi. I was introduced and came from behind the curtains. It was a wonderful experience to come forth and see all my *QE2* passenger friends. They were all my friends. I said a few words of thanks to the staff and crew on behalf of the passengers. I had now gained the confidence to do that!

After a brief explanation of the aria, I sang with enjoyment in my heart. This is what would console my soul. I have liked the *O Mio Babbino Caro* since I first heard it. After the applause, I sang the *Caro Nome*. That was the aria my brother liked. This I sang with all my heart. I received great applause. The end of the show was taken care of nicely. Brian asked all of the participants to get in a line and bow to the audience together. I thought this was a great ending. Thank you, Brian! You were great!

Passengers were now coming aboard for the return voyage to New York. I would have a table of new friends. It so happens that I feel sad when one table of friends leave. I can't seem to feel that the next group will be equally as nice. It is a trying time of the cruise. However, the new group of people were so compatible that before long I felt as though they had been with me for the whole trip. This group were mainly from the USA. One gentleman, however, was a retired pilot from

Manila. Another man was a superintendent of schools from Massachusetts. He was with his wife. There was a mother and daughter. They were from the mid west. We were a happy table.

For this return trip everything was very much the same. The theme of this sailing segment was "Les Maitres Cuisiniers de France". This meant that special attention was given to the gourmet foods served during the trip. Also the best chefs of France were to be honored at a presentation ceremony. I received in my cabin a small white chocolate menu embossed in dark chocolate. It looked so realistic that I didn't know that it was made of chocolate! When I did I thought it too artistic to eat! Each day the chefs gave a cooking demonstration. It was interesting particularly for those who do a lot of cooking. I don't fit into that category. However, I do like to cook.

One evening, as I was passing through the Chart Room, changing classes, Dr Nigel Roberts saw me come in and he asked me to sing. I had not had a chance to sing *La Vie En Rose* on this trip so I chose to sing it. David Moore, seated at the Queen Mary piano, quickly played an accompaniment for me. It was nice to be asked by the doctor. Thank you for asking, Dr Roberts!

It is relaxing to know that the trip is near its completion. We enjoyed the entertainment and the officers' cocktail party. It was now getting time to think about leaving. At this time we have a special dinner called Baked Alaska Night. The dining room is decorated with flags. At the precise moment all of the waiters enter the dining room carrying cakes of ice cream covered with whipped egg whites. Then above each is a sparkler. The lights are turned off and band music is played. It is very exciting. At dinner we are given a slice of the baked ice cream cake that is also covered with cherries! Our waitress was Sarah and the waiter was Peter. They gave me a folder of all of the menus of the transatlantic crossing. They put a handwritten note in it saying that they had enjoyed having the pleasure to serve me. Thank you Sarah and Peter. Yes, I kept it as a souvenir of your wonderful service and friendliness. Thank you both again!

Of course, it was the talent show that would be the last activity of the ship. This would need my undivided attention. I was confident enough to tell the wonderful people at my table that I would be participating. I don't usually tell, however, it seemed right to share it with them. I am very glad I did. I found out that the pilot at the table said he would video me being introduced and singing on stage. This was a really big help. So now, with a photographer and friends who knew about the show and the time of presentation, there was a totality about performing!

Andrew Graham signed in the performers for the show. He was the very nice social director from Australia. He signed me in and was telling me about placement. I told him that Brian Price had me enter from behind the stage curtain. He thought that was a good idea also. That pleased me!

The morning of the show, I practiced the arias I was to sing with the accompanist. We decided on two arias; *Un Bel Di Vedremo*, and *Caro Nome*. I decided to wear the pink gown, the rose crown, the opera length gloves and the pink fan! I carried the music, the camera, a small purse and the camcorder! Everything was in readiness.

The Master of Ceremonies was Andrew Graham. I waited behind the curtain for my cue. Then I came out on stage. He introduced me as coming from New Jersey. He said I would sing an aria from the opera Madame Butterfly called *Un Bel Di*. I was given the musical introduction and I sang. When I finished, the audience responded with a burst of applause. I could see some of my table companions in the fourth row clapping. Then Andrew came back on stage to introduce the next song. The applause was still being heard. A man in the front row said "She's good"! Andrew said, "Yes, she is and she usually gets a standing ovation." He then introduced the beautiful aria *Caro Nome*. I described the libretto a bit and then sang. I really felt great. I sang it just the way my vocal teacher at Rutgers University would have liked it sung. The applause was great and to my astonishment they were standing! I waved to everyone, particularly to my table of people that I could see clapping! I blew kisses and everyone looked happy on the *QE2*. With the memory of that ovation in mind I would like to conclude this saga of the high seas. Thank you one and all. I hope you have enjoyed this travelogue with me. I enjoyed sailing in words with you. I hope to see you again aboard the *QE2*. Until then, "Un Bacio". To all "a kiss".

Encore! That evening when I went to dinner, I found a surprise. My table companions had something for me. Yes, it was a beautiful bouquet of flowers. It had a note attached. It read, "Your fans, BRAVO!"